Praise for *Spotting Danger for Travelers* . . .

In his latest book *Spotting Danger for Travelers*, Gary Quesenberry draws on his nineteen years of experience as a federal air marshal to enlighten readers about the importance of situational awareness while traveling. Far from dry or clinical, Gary expertly weaves the technical aspects of situational aware-ness with personal stories and experiences to give the reader a deeper under-standing of the critical role awareness plays in personal safety. The result is a comprehensive yet easy-to-read guide that covers everything from setting up home security before you leave to post-travel considerations once you return home. So whether you're planning a big family vacation, solo business trip, or a quick weekend getaway, I highly recommend reading this book.

—Steven Pressfield, *New York Times* best-selling author, *The Legend of Bagger Vance*, *Gates of Fire*, *The War of Art*, among others

The term "Spotting Danger" is more relevant today than ever before in this increasingly dangerous world. Gary encapsulates why we need to be a lot more aware of our surroundings in simple and straightforward terms that everyone can understand and relate to.

—Rick Collins, founder and CEO of S.A.F.E. Inc.

Every environment is different, and what is normal in one place may be a warning sign in another. Unfamiliar environments have inherent risks, and understanding this can be the difference between a memorable trip or a tragic experience. *Spotting Danger for Travelers* is an important addition to the Spotting Danger series as it breaks down everything from preparation to pre-incident indicators in a sequence that is easy to follow and fun for an individual or for the whole family.

—Joseph Koury, US Army, Special Forces; federal agent, special agent in charge, Newark Field Office

Anyone who is a frequent traveler or is planning a domestic or international trip needs to read *Spotting Danger for Travelers*. Gary has taken the key fun-damentals of international safety operations and applied them to a realistic and sensible approach. Like Gary's other books in this series, he has presented principles of safety and security that are easily remembered and applied to enhance anyone's safety. I've had the honor of meeting and working with Gary at the Federal Air Marshal Service and co-instructed many of the topics he covers specifically in this book. Gary is spot on as he describes his pro-cesses and taking situational awareness on the road. Having been in some questionable security situations with Gary, I can attest that the guidance Gary offers in this book works. I've been fortunate to be one of the founders of two security companies that has worked with hundreds of churches across the United States. Many of the preparation and operational principles outlined in *Spotting Danger for Travelers* has been taught to church staff and volunteers serving on mission trips. The examples in this book brought back a lot of memories of my personal world travel but most important the reminder of the everchanging world and the need to be more vigilant then ever in our travels.

—Troy Szotkowski, founder and CEO of ACG
Security Consultants and National Tactical Security

Gary Quesenberry does it AGAIN! In this exceptionally well-written book, Gary effectively leverages his decades of experience in the counterterrorism and protection realm to succinctly communicate essential awareness fundamentals for traveling safely. The fourth book in Gary's awareness series *Spotting Danger for Travelers* seamlessly complements his previous work. This book is timely, especially given ever-evolving global threats that many societies are currently experiencing from the effects of geopolitical tension. Gary brilliantly articulates what is often lacking in the awareness industry: practical application of situational awareness and what to do before and during travel. As a personal protection instructor, my clients constantly request additional enhanced domain awareness resources and training for their day-to-day operations. I now have a "go to" resource I trust and rely on! Not only for them, but for my family and loved ones as well. Gary's ability to effectively communicate and tackle complex topics is sorely lacking in the awareness training industry. We should all be thankful for his commitment to equip others for success and for releasing another epic book on awareness. *Spotting Danger for Travelers* is a must-read for every traveler!

—Maury Abreu, CEO and chief instructor at Omega
Protective Concepts, former sergeant (United States
Marine Corps), federal correction officer (Federal
Bureau of Prisons), and supervisory federal air
marshal (Department of Homeland Security)

I have had the pleasure of knowing and working with Gary for twenty years. I always knew that he was a true expert and professional when it came to firearms and counter-terrorism tactics and principles. His lifetime of serving and protecting our nation has been poured into the Spotting Danger book series. His latest book *Spotting Danger for Travelers* is another useful and insightful work where Gary shares his expertise in keeping you safe while traveling at home or abroad. There are few people with more understanding about the dangers in this world than Gary. So if he is sharing, I highly recommend you listen! It may just save your life or the life of someone you love.

—Matthew Cubbler, thirty-year LEO, former
federal air marshal, author of *A Brother's Love: A
Memoir*, host of Two Dates and a Dash podcast

Before your next vacation or business trip, read *Spotting Danger for travelers* by Gary Quesenberry. You are responsible for your own safety, and the most important thing you can do to keep yourself and your loved ones safe is to practice effective situational awareness. Quesenberry not only teaches you how to do this better, he also shares what you should be aware of while traveling and ways to better pay attention to your surroundings and your own behaviors. I really like that Quesenberry highlights things to be aware of that many people might never consider. But once you read this book and think about it, you will remember what it has to say on every future trip and be safer because of it. Practicing what Quesenberry teaches in this straightforward and practical guide will allow you to get out and travel, see more of the world, and enjoy life safely.

—Alain B. Burrese, J.D., martial artist, author of *Survive a Shooting, Hard-Won Wisdom from the School of Hard Knocks, How to Protect Yourself by Developing a Fighter's Mindset,* among others

I've been a travel advisor and have owned my business for the last fifteen years. I've had the opportunity to travel by land, air, and sea. There are some points about safety I often stress to my clients, but Gary Quesenberry's book has all the questions and answers when it comes to safe traveling in an easy-to-read format. He teaches that the scenery may change, but one thing that remains constant is the ability to identify potential problems before they become a danger to your safety. The concept I thought most important, one he reiterates throughout the book, is how to grasp the "mechanics of situational awareness." His anecdotes are a big help in getting a grip on this concept. They are short, concise, sometimes amusing, but always to the point. You can imagine yourself in the situations that he describes. And you will certainly ask the question, "What would I do in this situation?"

I will recommend this book to my clients so that they will become more aware of the mechanics of situational awareness.

—Mary House, travel advisor, franchise owner, Cruise Planners

Once again Gary Quesenberry provides actionable information to keep his readers safe. This book builds upon other insights from his Spotting Danger series to inform travelers of what a predator sees in a tourist or business traveler, how to spot anomalies in new or unfamiliar cultures and locations, and how to manage every aspect of a trip from planning to safely returning home. Gary has compiled many useful tips into a comprehensive resource that helps his readers travel with confidence. As someone who frequently zigzags the country to host firearms training classes and matches, I will definitely put Gary's travel strategies to use on my upcoming trips.

—Robyn Sandoval, executive director for A Girl & A Gun Women's Shooting League

SPOTTING DANGER FOR TRAVELERS

SPOTTING DANGER FOR TRAVELERS

**Build Situational Awareness to
Keep Safe while Traveling**

GARY QUESENBERRY
Federal Air Marshal (Ret.)

YMAA Publication Center
Wolfeboro, NH

YMAA Publication Center, Inc.
PO Box 480
Wolfeboro, New Hampshire 03894
1-800-669-8892 • info@ymaa.com • www.ymaa.com

ISBN: 9781594399305 (print)
ISBN: 9781594399312 (ebook)
ISBN: 9781594399329 (hardcover)

Managing Editor: Doran Hunter
Cover design: Axie Breen
This book typeset in Sabon and Midiet

202300404

Photos by Shutterstock unless otherwise noted
Charts and graphs by the author

Publisher's Cataloging in Publication

Names: Quesenberry, Gary, author.
Title: Spotting danger for travelers : build situational awareness to keep safe while traveling / Gary Quesenberry.
Description: Wolfeboro, NH : YMAA Publication Center, [2023] | Includes bibliographical references and index.
Identifiers: ISBN: 9781594399305 (softcover) | 9781594399329 (hardcover) | 9781594399312 (ebook) | LCCN: 2022948944
Subjects: LCSH: Travel--Safety measures. | Vacations--Safety measures. | Situational awareness. | Safety education. | Self-protective behavior. | Self-preservation. | Self-defense. | Crime prevention--Psychological aspects. | Victims of crimes--Psychology. | Violence--Prevention. | BISAC: TRAVEL / Special Interest / Family. | SOCIAL SCIENCE / Violence in Society. | SPORTS & RECREATION / Martial Arts / General. | TRAVEL / Reference. | TRAVEL / Special Interest / Business.
Classification: LCC: G156.5.S43 Q47 2023 | DDC: 363.1/08--dc23

Note to Readers
Some identifying details have been changed to protect the privacy of individuals as well as the techniques and tactics employed by the Federal Air Marshal Service.

The authors and publisher of the material are NOT RESPONSIBLE in any manner whatsoever for any injury which may occur through reading or following the instructions in this manual.

The activities physical or otherwise, described in this manual may be too strenuous or dangerous for some people, and the reader(s) should consult a physician before engaging in them.

Warning: While self-defense is legal, fighting is illegal. If you don't know the difference you'll go to jail because you aren't defending yourself. You are fighting—or worse. Readers are encouraged to be aware of all appropriate local and national laws relating to self-defense, reasonable force, and the use of weaponry, and act in accordance with all applicable laws at all times. Understand that while legal definitions and interpretations are generally uniform, there are small—but very important—differences from state to state and even city to city. You need to know these differences. Neither the authors nor the publisher assumes any responsibility for the use or misuse of information contained in this book.

Nothing in this document constitutes a legal opinion nor should any of its contents be treated as such. While the authors believe that everything herein is accurate, any questions regarding specific self-defense situations, legal liability, and/or interpretation of federal, state, or local laws should always be addressed by an attorney at law.

When it comes to martial arts, self-defense, and related topics, no text, no matter how well written, can substitute for professional, hands-on instruction. These materials should be used for academic study only.

Printed in Canada

For the adventurers
May you always have the road beneath your feet,
and your eyes on the horizon.

Contents

"Got no time for spreading roots
The time has come to be gone
And though our health we drank a thousand times
It's time to ramble on."

—Led Zeppelin

Foreword

by Tony Blauer

"TRY NOT TO STICK OUT LIKE A TOURIST"—we've all heard that expression, but how exactly is it possible to be a tourist and not look like one? If you're traveling, you're by definition a tourist. You will be taking in the sights and navigating the culture of a place that is probably unfamiliar to you. How could you not stand out?

Before I share more thoughts on the importance of Gary's book, let me tell you a little bit about my background just to give you some perspective. I've been studying violence, fear, and aggression for over forty years. Way back in the 80s, I realized that most self-defense methods are designed for *after* the fight has started. Think about it. How to block a punch. How to escape a choke. How to counter a headlock. How to perform a gun disarm. All of these techniques and most self-defense moves are deployed after the initial attack!

That intrigued me. Why wouldn't people want to learn how to intercept an attack or, better yet, completely avoid the confrontation? And that's how I began redesigning self-defense so it was behaviorally based and effective in the real world. I started by redefining the term "self-defense" entirely. This is the old definition, according to *Merri-am-Webster's Collegiate Dictionary*:

self-defense / self-di-'fen(t)s / n. **1:** *a plea of justification for the use of force or for homicide*
    2: *the act of defending oneself, one's property, or a close relative*

Official definitions for self-defense don't mention situational aware-ness, avoidance, or de-escalation, which together form the bedrock of Gary's message. Here is the SPEAR System® definition:

The decision to choose safety when danger is imminent.

Simple, complete, holistic, and inclusive. It allows us to run away, and it also allows us to charge the threat. The scenario will always dictate which one.

But let me ask you this: wouldn't you avoid violence altogether if given the choice? And that's why all of Gary's books are so important. Each book teaches you how to mentally prepare and avoid conflict and confrontations. I won't try to impress you by using the term "reticular activating system" (RAS) in a sentence, but I will tell you that analyzing scenarios and mentally reviewing options and contin-gencies will dramatically improve your reaction time. That alone is reason enough to follow the guidelines in *Spotting Danger for Travelers*.

If you think about possible scenarios in advance and formulate plans to avoid and manage conflict, you will not only enhance your survivability, you are also much more likely to enjoy your trip because you'll be able to relax more knowing you're prepared. And that is exactly what Gary's books, especially this one, will help you to do.

Some of the content seems obvious when you read it, and you may think, "Ah, this is common sense!" But I assure you it's not. That's why this book is so important. Here's a real-world example. I'm a personal defense expert who travels all over the world. I'm experienced in both sides of the toolbox, from situational awareness to extreme close-quarter tactics. Several years ago, I was in Dallas to work on a show with retired Navy SEAL Dom Raso. When I finally arrived after a few flight delays, I was starving and needed a good steak. I searched restaurants in the area on my smartphone, found what looked like a good one, and started to walk toward the location. After about ten minutes, I realized I was looking down at my phone as I walked and then looking up to make sure I was going in the right direction. It was getting dark and my surroundings were unfamiliar. And I was beginning to realize that the nice area near the hotel had given way to a not-so-nice area.

At that moment, I realized I looked like a tourist. Worse, I had compromised my situational awareness because I was holding my phone, making me look lost and unsure of where I was going. On top of that, my senses in general and my peripheral vision in particular were compromised by having so much of my attention focused on my device. My head movement and the glow from the little screen told any opportunistic criminal I was the tourist Gary warns us not to be.

This sudden realization made me pause and tune in to my senses. I listened, then looked. Everything felt fine (remember, listening to your intuition is a huge part of personal safety). So I stepped off the sidewalk, away from the dark bushes, and headed into the road where the streetlights provided illumination, allowing me to see more and scan my surroundings. I was safe. I took one more quick look at the directions on the map, memorized the next part of the walk, then put it in my pocket so my hands (and attention) were free, changed my pace, and got the hell out of that neighborhood.

I shared this story because I wanted to remind you that SMEs (subject matter experts) are human too. Had I read Gary's book, I'd have spoken to the front desk, asked for information about the area, and then taken an Uber since it was getting dark. That would have been a much safer approach than traveling on foot through a sketchy area while distracted like a typical tourist.

This book will help you stack the odds overwhelmingly in favor of your safety, especially if you actually do the exercises too. And while you will hopefully never need to activate Plan B, you'll improve your reaction time if worse ever does come to worst.

So have fun as a tourist. Just make sure to read Gary's book and learn not to stick out like one.

Tony Blauer
Founder, SPEAR System®
Blauer Training Systems

Introduction

I WORKED AS A FEDERAL AIR MARSHAL for close to nineteen years. Although I can't disclose details about our missions or the flights I covered, I can say that over the course of my domestic and international deployments, I logged a total of 2.4 million aviation miles. Despite the hardships we endured and the unforeseen changes to come, I still take great pride in the work we did. I jokingly told people that I was in the air more than most birds, but that was the job, and I loved it.

In the early months of 2020, news outlets started reporting on a new virus called COVID-19 and how it could possibly impact air travel. No big deal, right? I had flown through viral outbreaks before: West Nile, SARS, H1N1, and Zika, to name a few. Like most Americans, I assumed we'd get the standard safety warnings, news bulletins, and constant reminders to wash our hands. But this time, things went a little further than that. On March 10th, 2020, I stepped off a flight from Amsterdam, Netherlands. The next day, the World Health Organization (WHO) declared COVID-19 a highly contagious and deadly global pandemic. International travel came to a halt, and citizens around the world were urged to stay indoors. Because I had just come from a city where COVID-19 cases were on the rise, I was removed from the flight schedule and placed in quarantine for fourteen days. "Fine, I'll sit at home for a couple of weeks and catch up on some yard work while this whole thing blows over." Although I didn't know it at the time, I had just taken my last international flight as a federal air marshal. By October of that same year, I had retired from service and moved back to my hometown in Virginia. There, I waited along with the rest of the world for COVID to run its course.

According to the World Tourism Organization (UNWTO), there was a 72-percent drop in international arrivals worldwide between January and October of 2020.[1] That number represents 900 million fewer international travelers than the year before and a loss of over 935 billion dollars in revenue from tourism. Those numbers have had a devastating effect on the global economy. On an individual level, many people found it hard to cope with the feelings of isolation and hopelessness created by mandated stay-at-home orders. According to a December 2020 survey by the US Census Bureau, medical professionals started to see a global "surge" in reported cases of anxiety and depression. Forty-two percent of people in the United States reported symptoms of depressive disorders in that month alone, a 31-percent increase over the previous year. On top of that, the closing of businesses deemed to be nonessential created significant financial hardship for families all over the world.

In all of the chaos created by COVID-19, the vast majority of people simply kept their heads down and did whatever they could to get through this pandemic with minimal impact on their health and well-being. It's been a long and difficult road since the onset of the pandemic, but the good news is that things are finally starting to turn around. As I write these words, the majority of COVID restrictions

---

1. UNWTO "Impact Assessment of the COVID-19 Outbreak on International Travel, " https://www.unwto.org/impact-assessment-of-the-covid-19-outbreak-on-international-tourism.

have been lifted, and things are starting to get back to normal. Businesses have reopened, children have returned to school, and thank God, travel is now back on the table. Whether it's for a business trip, a long weekend, or a full-blown family vacation, we're all feeling the need to break away from our pandemic-mandated constraints and strike out in search of a little adventure. It's been a very long wait, but it's time to lace up those traveling shoes and hit the road again. Vacations, weekend getaways, and even business trips can offer experiences that are exciting, educational, and sometimes even awe-inspiring, but they can also be dangerous. It's not my intention to put a damper on your post-pandemic excitement, but leaving home to travel through unfamiliar territory does come with some level of risk, and you need to be prepared for that.

In the year prior to COVID-19, we saw a significant increase in crimes targeting tourists; those included street scams, robberies, kidnappings, and even murder, but the commission of those crimes dropped dramatically during the lockdown period. It's safe to say that even criminals decided to take those stay-at-home orders seriously. Although the more violent crimes against vacationers are less common, there has always been a need to exercise sound judgment and good situational awareness, even when you're supposed to be relaxing. That's especially important now that families are starting to vacation again. As domestic and international destinations begin to loosen their travel restrictions, there's the potential that crimes targeting tourists will rebound to at least their previous levels, if not higher. For that reason, it's imperative that we reassess our individual levels of security and beef up our situational awareness before we start planning our next big getaway.

In my first book, *Spotting Danger Before It Spots You, Build Situational Awareness to Stay Safe,* I covered the basic concepts of situational awareness and how your body language can signal weakness to predatory criminals. You learned that by simply lifting your head up and looking around you change the way you are perceived by others and can significantly increase your levels of awareness and safety. Those same concepts apply even when you're on vacation. Regardless of your location, criminals tend to stick to specific patterns of behavior; we call those patterns "pre-incident indicators." The ability to accurately predict the actions of others based on the early recognition of those indicators can help you avoid violent situations before they have a chance to manifest. It is crucial to know how predators choose their victims and to be able to establish behavioral baselines, identify baseline anomalies, and harden your personal defenses, but to make such knowledge and skills part of your routine, especially while traveling, takes practice and willpower.

In this fourth book in the Spotting Danger series I break travel safety down into three phases:

1. The first phase, PRE-DEPARTURE, covers preparations such as researching your destination, home security, and establishing a support system while you're away. Relaxing and minimizing distractions on vacation will be a lot easier if you're confident in the fact that everything is safe and secure back home.

2. The second phase, TRAVEL, will cover travel safety on the road and in the air. The scenery may constantly be changing, but keeping your guard up, even while in transit, is a crucial element of personal safety.

3. Finally, phase three, ARRIVAL, will cover the things that need to happen once you've made it to your destination. Knowing what to look out for when you're on the ground, how to react when things go wrong, and how to maintain communications with your family and friends are critical security considerations and can mean the difference between a fun-filled adventure and a traumatic experience.

Before we begin, I think it's important to look at some facts and statistics that tie into the motivating factors behind the commission of crime. The four elements that most often motivate criminal actions are money, territory, ego, and emotion. Although each of these factors can come into play during a vacation, money tops the list when it comes to targeting tourists. According to the US Travel Association, domestic and international vacationers spend nearly 1.1 trillion dollars annually in the US alone. The average American couple will spend $581 on a single domestic weekend trip. In comparison, international travelers will spend up to $3,500 during a twelve-day vacation.[2] Those numbers exclude travel costs such as fuel and airfare and increase significantly depending on the number of family members you have with you. That's a lot of money, and any time there's that much cash involved, you can guarantee there will be someone nearby looking to take advantage of an unsuspecting tourist.

Aside from the money factor, territory can also play a significant role in the targeting of tourists. That's why planning and area familiarization are so essential when it comes to maintaining your safety. During my career as a federal air marshal, one of my favorite things to do was to lace up my shoes and head out on a long walk through a new city. Europe, especially, is filled with museums, mountains, beaches, massive cathedrals, and castles; I wanted to see it all. While traveling, I quickly learned that my safety depended upon more than just my wits and training; it was imperative that I thoroughly familiarize myself with my surroundings to avoid ending up in areas where my presence may be unwelcome. There are hundreds of resources for travelers that can help with this part of your trip planning. We'll go into more detail about this later, and I've included a "travel resources" section in the appendix to help you with your research.

After money and territory, there's ego and emotion. These two factors are ever present regardless of where you may find yourself. On vacation, both can be amplified and become liabilities to your safety, especially when you mix alcohol into the equation. I can't even begin to list the number of fights I've seen erupt between locals and tourists

2. https://www.ustravel.org/system/files/media_root/document/Research_Fact-Sheet_US-Travel-and-Tourism-Overview.pdf.

just because of ego and emotion. A good friend and coworker of mine had his leg completely shattered during a fight that broke out over a World Cup soccer match. He was on a mission with his team overseas, and they decided to grab a bite to eat at a local pub where the match was being aired. Soccer fans from all over the world had made their way to the pub, and it was so crowded my friend had to take up a position on the patio just outside the entrance. During the match, words were exchanged between some English and South American soccer fans, egos were bruised, and emotions got out of control. My friend wasn't directly involved in the fight. He was positioned just outside the entrance with his back to the door. His thought was, "I'd rather see who was coming in as opposed to who was leaving." When the fight spilled outside, he was taken by surprise. He was able to fight off the first person who rushed him from the door but the crowd that quickly followed crushed him against the patio railing. Luckily, his teammates were able to pull him to safety. They were also familiar enough with the area to get him out of harm's way and seek proper medical attention. Now, nineteen years later, my friend still walks with a slight limp, but things could have been much worse. All because some people in a crowd couldn't control their egos or emotions.

I don't tell these stories to strike fear into the hearts of travelers; I tell them to help raise awareness. Although most vacationers can travel freely without ever falling victim to crime, there is always the potential for danger, especially in a post-pandemic world. I started writing the Spotting Danger series so everyone can develop a solid foundation of situational awareness and give themselves the advantage of being able to preemptively spot danger, quickly implement escape plans, and take control of their own safety. I know from experience that following the techniques I've outlined in this book can give you that advantage. So read on, and do so with the knowledge that what you learn here will help to keep you safe, regardless of where your travels may take you.

PHASE ONE——Pre-Departure

"Before anything else, preparation is the key to success."
—ALEXANDER GRAHAM BELL

1

Planning Your Trip

So, YOU'VE DECIDED to go on vacation. Good for you! Everyone needs to get away from time to time and take a much-needed break from the doldrums of their everyday routine. Let's face it, work can be a drag, and getting away on vacation is a great way to recharge your batteries and refocus on the things that are most important: family, friends, fun. It sounds good, right? Of course it does, but when you're planning a successful getaway, you have to think about more than just the fun stuff; you also have to consider your personal safety and the safety of those you're traveling with. This is where situational awareness comes into play.

I define situational awareness as the ability to identify and process environmental cues for the purpose of accurately predicting the actions of others. It's not an overly complicated process, and you don't have to be a soldier, police officer, or federal air marshal to master it. In fact, you really only need four things:

1. An understanding of various environments
2. The ability to differentiate between normal and abnormal behaviors within those environments

3. An understanding of how variations in those behaviors could possibly impact your safety
4. The ability to develop plans for avoidance or escape based on what you see

Sounds easy, right? Well, it is, but it takes focus and practice to make it a natural part of your daily routine. If you think about it, you're more than likely doing these things already; for example, you're driving down the street and coming to a four-way intersection. Another car is approaching from your left. It looks as if the driver is distracted by someone in the backseat and isn't slowing down. Based on what you observe in that situation, you can pretty accurately predict the outcome. The driver will likely miss the stop sign and blow through the intersection, so you remain in place and patiently wait for them to pass. That's it. You just used situational awareness as a means of ensuring your own safety. In most cases, it's that simple, but things tend to get a little more complicated when it comes to predatory violence, especially when you find yourself in unfamiliar surroundings. We're going to get into those differences later on, but for now, let's discuss why the early detection of potential security risks is so important.

Practicing situational awareness dramatically increases your chances of spotting dangerous situations before they happen and sharpens your ability to predict the actions of others. Ideally, this process of identifying and analyzing risks takes place well before you decide to leave the house. When you're preparing for a trip away, the first step in identifying potential problems begins in the planning phase. Proper planning requires more than just picking a vacation spot and packing a bag. It requires some in-depth research and preparation if you want to make sure your getaway is both safe and enjoyable. We can break this planning stage down into three primary segments:

1. **Threat assessment:** This is the process of using personal and online resources to evaluate the threat level within a particular environment. We'll cover this in-depth in the next chapter.

2. **Itinerary development:** This is nothing more than preplanning your activities to maximize your time away from home. I won't spend much time on this portion because not everyone plans every little detail in advance. Plus, itineraries can vary wildly depending on your individual tastes and personality. What's important to remember is not to be completely rigid in your planning. Always be prepared to "flex" your plans should the need arise. This need to adjust can stem from unforeseen issues back at home or security concerns at your destination. Travel guides and internet searches won't help you uncover every possible danger in advance, so it's always best to have backup plans should one of your activities fall through. This is known as contingency planning.

3. **Contingency planning:** As the old saying goes, "If something can go wrong, it will." No one likes to think that way when planning their vacation, but it's crucial to develop standardized emergency responses well in advance of your travel. Things like medical emergencies, separation from family members, lost communications, and the risks of getting stranded all have to be considered. We'll cover this in more detail in chapter seventeen.

J. R. R. Tolkien once wrote, "It does not do to leave a live dragon out of your calculations if you live near one." Granted, this quote may be from a story about an old wizard and a questing Hobbit, but it makes a great point. When it comes to travel, you have to identify and consider your "dragons," or those things that could pose a significant danger to you over the course of your journey. That's why this planning stage is so important. Once you've picked your destination, it's time to begin your targeted research on that location and identify any security risks that you may need to consider. This process of collecting information on a particular area is referred to as a threat assessment.

Key Points:

- Situational awareness is the ability to identify and process environmental cues for the purpose of accurately predicting the actions of others.
- For situational awareness to be most effective you need four things:
  1. An understanding of your environment
  2. The ability to differentiate between normal and abnormal behaviors within that environment
  3. An understanding of how variations in those behaviors could possibly impact your safety
  4. The ability to develop plans for avoidance or escape based on what you see within your environment
- Practicing situational awareness dramatically increases your chances of spotting dangerous situations before they happen and sharpens your ability to predict the actions of others.
- We can break the planning stage of your trip down into three primary segments:
  1. Threat assessment
  2. Itinerary development
  3. Contingency planning

2

Conducting a Threat Assessment

A THREAT ASSESSMENT is a process of determining the level of risk associated with a particular region and making decisions based on the severity of that risk while considering your defenses and vulnerabilities. This may sound a little complicated, but we're going to keep things nice and simple here. We're planning a vacation after all, not conducting a hostage rescue. Unless you're already familiar with your destination, threat assessments will require a little targeted research. Consider this portion of your planning phase to be "intelligence gathering." For the purposes of this book, we'll use two specific sources to gather our information: open-source intelligence (OSINT) and human intelligence (HUMINT).

OSINT can be derived from information that is readily available to the general public. You don't have to have a top-secret clearance to access Google, so that's always a good place to start. But be careful. There's a serious threat of information overload when you're using the Internet to gather intelligence. To avoid confusion, keep your searches specific and relevant to your planning, and always stick to credible sources.

During a threat assessment, you're just trying to answer one simple question: "Is the area I want to visit safe?" For foreign destinations, a good place to start is the US Department of State website. I've used this resource for years to do personal research on foreign locations. There, you can read travel advisories and alerts for the places you plan on visiting, review entry/exit and visa requirements, and gather a lot of important information about local laws and customs, medical care facilities, and transportation safety. I recommend the State Department site as a starting point for your research because it considers each traveler's individual circumstances and personal safety concerns. Here's a brief list of the specific types of travelers the State Department addresses.

- Adventure travelers
- US travelers in Europe
- High-risk area travelers
- Journalist travelers
- Faith-based travelers
- Pilgrimage travelers (Hajj, Umrah)
- US students abroad
- Cruise ship travelers

- LGBTQ travelers
- Women travelers
- Travelers with disabilities
- Older travelers

That's a pretty thorough list, but the benefits provided by the site don't end there. The State Department also allows travelers to enroll in STEP (Smart Traveler Enrollment Program). Enrollment is free and the benefits are incredible. Here are a few things you can expect once you've completed your enrolment.

Get Country-Specific Travel Advisories Delivered to Your Inbox

When you have a Smart Traveler Enrollment account, you enter your country destinations and get reports that detail current social climate and security threats before you ever leave home. While traveling, you'll get updated fact sheets and emergency messages for the countries you're visiting delivered right to your email. These real-time updates give you all the information you need to make sound desicions during your planning.

Expedite Passport Recovery and Emergency Services

Smart travelers make passport security their number-one priority while traveling, but unexpected things still happen despite your best efforts. With your STEP account, your passport and identification information will be securely stored in case your passport is lost, stolen, or destroyed while traveling, making it easier for the American embassies to help you in any kind of emergency.

Assist in Your Own Evacuation

With a Smart Traveler Enrollment account, you'll be in a database of US citizens visiting a particular country in the event of a natural disaster or security threat. Having this connection can prove invaluable in a time of crisis. Past emergencies include the evacuation of American citizens following the outbreak of war and civil unrest, in places like Afghanistan and Ukraine.

Receive Urgent Information from Home

Occasionally, the crisis is on the other end of travel: home. Your Smart Traveler Enrollment account provides a means for consulates across the globe to contact you when there is an emergency. While it's great to escape the day-to-day with travel, the smart traveler always has a backup means of communication in case of a real emergency.[3]

In addition, groups or organizations can create an account and upload a spreadsheet with contact details for multiple travelers. Aside from the State Department site, the Internet is packed with valuable resources for vacationers, from travel blogs, local news sites, and weather trackers to review apps like Yelp and Trip Advisor. Travelers can search popular locations, find restaurants, and plot their sightseeing destinations, all from the comfort of their living room.

Another resource I frequently use is Google Earth, which is fantastic for mapping out routes, determining distance to and from points of interest, and discovering those hard-to-find places that everyone talks about but no one can seem to find. For example, below, you'll find an aerial photo of my favorite restaurant in Athens, Greece, The Smile Café. The top photo is a street-level view of the cafe, and the image on the bottom is a marked route from The Smile Café to the Temple of Zeus. You get a clear picture of the area around the café as well as routes to and from, plus you can mark out distances to your next destination.

As you can see, the route is clearly marked, and the distance is notated in the upper right-hand corner. Keep in mind that Google Earth isn't updated very often. In fact, the average map is only updated every one to three years, so consider that when you're planning out your routes.

Another great OSINT resource if you're traveling internationally is the CIA World Fact Book, which is released annually and offers

---

3. https://www.us-passport-service-guide.com/4-Benefits-of-the-Smart-Traveler-Enrollment-Program-STEP.html.

complete and up-to-date information on the world's nations. It covers everything from infrastructure issues with communications and transportation to political conditions and the likelihood of civil unrest. You can also find essential facts about population demographics, crime rates, weather patterns, and police capabilities. It's one of the most comprehensive fact books available to the general public, so I highly recommend picking up a copy before your next trip overseas. These same resources are also available to domestic travelers. Remember that all of your research and planning should be conducted well in advance of your vacation. That way, you can free your mind up to be better focused on your surroundings when you finally arrive on-site.

HUMINT is information gathered from credible human sources. This one's easy. All you need to do is find people who have been where you intend to go and ask them questions about their trip. People love talking about their vacation experiences, so be prepared for a bit of information overload. Take what is most relevant to your concerns and learn as much as you can about the area you'll be visiting. Just remember to keep things simple; here are a few questions you may want to ask:

- Where did you stay?
- Was your hotel clean, well secured, and convenient for public transportation?
- What was the biggest difference in how people live there compared to here?
- Was there a language barrier, and how did that affect your ability to communicate effectively with other people?
- What is the most common form of transportation there?
- Was there anything you did or saw that you wish you'd skipped?
- What did you pack that came in handy?
- What do you wish you had packed that you didn't?
- Was it easy to find and buy things you needed along the way?
- Did you notice any cultural norms that would be helpful for someone to know before visiting?
- What do you wish you knew before you even booked your flight?
- Did you experience any safety concerns on your trip, whether related to the destination itself or the actual traveling?
- If so, what should people be aware of to avoid those concerns?
- What websites or services did you find the most helpful for planning/booking your trip?

- What advice would you give someone going there for the first time?
- What was the most enjoyable or relaxing part of your trip?
- Would you go back?
- If so, what would you do differently?

This may seem like a lot to ask, but the information you compile may be relevant to your safety and should be gathered from more than one source to avoid biased opinions. Just be sure to listen intently, consider how what you're hearing impacts your travel plans, and adjust accordingly should the need arise. It's a good idea to jot down some notes as well. Those may come in handy when you brief your traveling companions about your plans.

Key Points:
- A threat assessment is a process of determining the level of risk associated with a particular region and making decisions based on the severity of that risk while considering your defenses and vulnerabilities.
- During this portion of your planning, you will gather information from two sources:
  - Open-source intelligence (OSINT)
  - Human intelligence (HUMINT)
- OSINT can be derived from information that is readily available to the general public. I recommend using resources such as:
  - Google
  - The State Department website
  - Apps like Yelp and Trip Advisor
  - Google Earth
  - The CIA World Fact Book
- HUMINT is information gathered from credible human sources.
- When talking to people who have been to the area you plan on visiting ask questions that will give you a fuller picture what to expect once you arrive.

3

Home Security and Support

NOW THAT YOU'VE COMPLETED the threat assessment, you have a much better idea of what issues may arise during your travels and what risks you could face at your final destination. If you're anything like me, simply walking out the front door and kicking off a worry-free vacation isn't quite that easy. I sometimes have problems backing out of the driveway without worrying about what's happening inside the house. Did I leave the coffeepot on? Was the back door locked? Did I remember to set the alarm? Questions like this can nag at us to the point of exhaustion and cause us to lose focus on the fact that we're supposed to be enjoying ourselves. That's why establishing a reliable support system back home is so important. It's an essential element of your planning phase if you really want to forget about things for a while and just unwind.

Let's start with the basics. The first thing you'll need to establish is a primary point of contact at home. Whether it's a family member, a close personal friend, or a trusted neighbor, this person will be the one responsible for keeping an eye on things while you're away. Although it's a good idea to have one person as a primary contact, you can recruit as much help as you feel you'll need to keep things running smoothly. This network of family, friends, and neighbors will be crucial to the enjoyment of your vacation, so choose wisely.

According to an FBI crime statistics report from 2017, there were approximately three burglaries every minute in the United States. That adds up to about 3,757 burglaries a day. Over 70 percent of those burglaries take place when no one is at home, between the hours of 6:00 am and 6:00 pm. Burglary rates are also shown to be much higher during the summer months when families are away on vacation. Given these statistics, it's safe to assume that you are much less likely to be burglarized if everyone thinks you're still at home. Your support system will play a critical role in this area. Regardless of whether you're home or not, the people you recruit to help out while you're away can assist in keeping your house look occupied and active, making it much less attractive to potential burglars.

In 2015 the Allen, Texas, police department arrested Michael Shayne Durden, a notorious burglar who had committed approximately eighty robberies in Allen and the surrounding areas. Facing up to thirty years in prison for his crimes, Durden agreed to an interview with the Allen PD spokesperson, Sgt. Jon Felty, to discuss his methods. The interview aimed to help other homeowners avoid becoming targets of burglary. The resulting video, "Inside the Mind of a Thief—Burglar Confessions," can be found on YouTube and gives us an incredible look into the mindset of a career criminal.[4] It also gives us insight into what things work and don't work when it comes to protecting our homes.

When Durden wasn't robbing homes, he was a paid personal trainer. His preferred method for casing a neighborhood was to lace up his running shoes and jog through affluent subdivisions looking for the perfect target. When asked what kept him away from specific communities, Durden quickly responded, "Nosey neighbors . . . There's been so many times I've gone and cased a neighborhood and stayed away from that neighborhood because it was obvious to me that there were

---

4. "Inside the Mind of a Thief—Burglar Confessions," https://www.youtube.com/watch?v=DtwD-c9hn58.

people out walking, and they had the VIP program, and it makes a lot of difference. It'll totally deter me from going anywhere near that neighborhood because I don't want ever to enter into a situation where I'm confronted by anyone. That's the whole reason for casing the homes. I'm not a home invader who would go in and tie people up. I'm a thief."

Durden's interview makes it obvious that vigilant neighbors, neighborhood watches, and active communities are fantastic deterrents to crime. If you live in an area that participated in these programs, you're already one step ahead in terms of home security. But what if you don't live in such a neighborhood? What if you live in a more remote area and structured watch programs aren't available? What's the best way to maintain the appearance of an active household and minimize the likelihood that your home is targeted while you're away? This is where your support system comes into play.

Over the years, I've had the opportunity to break away from work-related travel and get away with my family from time to time. The first step I always took in my travel preparations was to tap into my support system to help me maintain the appearance of an active home. Now, thanks to "smart" technologies and app-controlled home security devices, it's way easier to make it look like someone is home even when you're gone. Here are a few of the methods I would always use:

1. Stop the newspaper and mail, or ask someone in your support team to pick them up. Nothing gives away the fact that you're out of town quicker than a pile of old newspapers in the yard or a mailbox stuffed full of envelopes. Make sure someone will be available to collect your mail and keep everything cleared out at least three or four days a week.

2. If you're leaving your car at home, make sure it's parked in the garage. If you leave your car in the driveway unmoved for several days at a time, that's a dead giveaway that no one is home.

3. Ask a friend or neighbor to park a car in your driveway from time to time to make your house look active.

4. Use timers or "smart home" devices to control the lighting. Turn lights or televisions on in different rooms from time to time so that it looks like someone is there at night.

5. Keep your lawn maintained. Have someone do the mowing and trimming while you're away, or hire a landscaping service. If it's winter, make sure someone keeps the driveway and sidewalks cleared.

6. Have someone water any exterior plants. Dead plants are another indicator that someone's been gone for a while.

These are just a few of the things you can do to help maintain the illusion that your home is active, even when you're not there. As we learned from Mr. Durden, the appearance of an occupied home is a fantastic way to safeguard against criminals, but there are other things you should be doing just to be on the safe side.

According to a study conducted by getsafe.com, the average burglar takes eight to ten minutes to strip whatever they need from your home. The speed of these attacks comes from the fact that professional burglars have a "wish list," or items they know they can quickly sell for cash. By understanding how burglars think and what they're looking for, you can better protect your belongings while you're away. Here's a list of the top items criminals are looking for once they make entry into your home.

- **Cash:** This one is the most obvious. Criminals love cash because it eliminates the amount of exposure they're subjected to when they sell or pawn the things they steal, plus it's untraceable and easily carried away.
- **Electronics:** Small electronics are the primary targets here. Things like laptops, gaming systems, and tablets are easy to conceal in a small bag and easy to walk away with. If the thief thinks they have more time, or there are no neighbors to keep watch, they are more likely to take their time and go for the bigger items like televisions, sound systems, and desktop computers.
- **Guns:** Guns are easy to walk away with, and they bring a good price on the street. There's a high demand for firearms among professional criminals, so they can generally be gotten rid of quickly.
- **Jewelry:** Jewelry is easy to find and easy to get rid of. The quicker a criminal can get rid of stolen items and convert them to cash, the less likely they will get caught.
- **Personal identification:** This one may be less obvious. Still, it's a big find for thieves if they can obtain enough of your personal information to either steal your identity or sell that information to the highest bidder.
- **Medication:** Given the opioid epidemic we're currently facing, medications are a very likely target for burglars. Medications are easily hidden and transported, and they can be quickly converted to cash.

Now that you know what they're looking for, what's the best way to protect your personal belongings? One way to safeguard your things is to understand how burglars think and what routes they generally take once they're inside your home. Most people keep valuables in their bedrooms, so burglars tend to make that their first stop. They usually scan dressers and easily accessible drawers for cash and jewelry. Once that's done, they may check the closets looking for guns, money, expensive items of clothing, or even a conveniently located suitcase or gym bag to help transport their findings away from the house. The medicine cabinet is also a top priority when searching the master bathroom. The kids' bedrooms are often the best places to find gaming systems, computers, iPads, and other high-end electronics. After that, there's the home office. Those are great places to find small safes and personal information. If there's time, the burglar may make a quick trip to the basement or garage. Power tools and other small items are easily transported and easy to pawn. By knowing where to find the things they're looking for, criminals can make quick work of an unsecured house and keep their exposure to a minimum.

Now the question presents itself: if my support system fails and a burglar targets my house, how do I best protect my belongings? As the old saying goes, "The best offense is a good defense." Criminals and terrorists alike tend to divide their targets into two groups: hard targets and soft targets. This concept applies to both people and places. A place, such as your home, can be considered a hard target when there are apparent countermeasures in place that would deter a possible attack, such as fences, cameras, and barriers that discourage unwanted entry. A few things you can do before leaving home to harden your defenses are as follows:

- Add motion-activated floodlights around your home. There's nothing thieves hate more than well-lit areas, so I always recommend floodlights on each corner of the house.
- Add a video-and-audio-recording doorbell such as "Ring" or "Nest." These are relatively inexpensive and go a long way in keeping unwanted visitors away from the front door.

- Home alarm systems monitor door openings as well as glass breakage. Audible alarms are a great deterrent, but the monitored systems that include a police response are preferable.
- Add warning signs near easily accessible doors and windows to let potential criminals know that your home is being monitored.

Once these exterior defenses are in place, it's also essential to have some interior defenses as a backup. I've always encouraged people to purchase a large home safe, preferably one that weighs over three hundred pounds. The small document safes that some people own are great, but they can be easily located and carried off. I personally own a 1,200-pound safe that I move all of our valuables to when I know we're going to be away for more than a day or two. If someone were to make it into my house, they'd have a hard time finding anything valuable that could be easily carried off.

So those are the three primary tools you'll need to protect your home while you're away.

1. Having a good idea of how criminals work and what items they may target can help you secure the things you want to protect.
2. Reinforcing your outer defenses will help give the appearance of a hard target and make your house less appealing to criminals.
3. A robust support system will help to make your home look active and lived in.

Now that these measures are in place, you can relax and enjoy your time away, knowing that everything back home is safe and secure. But first, it's time to talk to your co-travelers about some of the security concerns you identified during your threat assessment, so break out those notes.

Key Points:

- The first thing you'll need to establish is a primary point of contact at home.

- According to an FBI crime statistics report from 2017, there were approximately three burglaries every minute in the United States. That adds up to about 3,757 burglaries a day. Over 70 percent of those burglaries take place when no one is at home between the hours of 6:00 am and 6:00 pm.
- Here are a few common methods to make your house appear to be occupied, even while you're away:
  - Stop the newspaper and mail.
  - If you're leaving your car at home, make sure it's parked in the garage.
  - Ask a friend or neighbor to park a car in your driveway from time to time to make your house look active.
  - Use timers or "smart home" devices to control the lighting.
  - Keep your lawn maintained, or driveways and sidewalks cleared of snow.
  - Have someone water any exterior plants.
- The top items criminals are looking for once they make entry into your home.
  - Cash
  - Electronics
  - Guns
  - Jewelry
  - Personal identification
  - Medication
- A few things you can do before leaving home to harden your defenses are as follows:
  - Add motion-activated floodlights around your home.
  - Add a video-and-audio-recording doorbell such as "Ring" or "Nest."
  - Add warning signs near easily accessible doors and windows to let potential criminals know that your home is being monitored.

4

Intel Briefing

AT THIS POINT, you've thoroughly researched your destination and collected all the relevant information you need regarding travel and safety. If you're traveling alone, you're all set, but if you're traveling with family or friends, it's time to sit down together and discuss the intel you've collected. It's crucial that everyone in your party understand the area you'll be visiting, have a general idea of the itinerary, and know what safety precautions need to be considered during each phase of travel. In the Federal Air Marshal Service, this is known as the "intelligence briefing." Keep in mind that law enforcement intelligence briefings can be long, exhaustive, and downright dull. If you're traveling with others, that's no way to kick off their vacation experience, so let's stick with the basics and keep things on a lighter note.

If you found information relevant to the group's safety during your threat assessment, now's the time to discuss it. It's imperative everyone understands what areas you'll be visiting, what the likelihood of danger will be, and in what regions close contact and frequent communication will be critical. For instance, Spring Fest in Munich, Germany, is crowded, bustling, and abounds with vibrant colors, games, and dancing. The air is filled with music and the smell of freshly baked pretzels, and there's plenty of drinking and shouting. People will also purposefully try to sidetrack you and draw you into their group of merrymakers. When walking through all this, it's easy to become distracted and even separated from your group, so emphasizing the importance of sticking together and maintaining communications in a situation like this should definitely be included in your briefing.

Spring Fest, Munich, Germany
(photo by author)

Aside from the obvious safety concerns, the intel briefing is also a great time to consider the rest of the group's wants, needs, and opinions. Everyone has different personalities after all, and if you want your vacation to be enjoyed by the entire group, you're going to need to discuss everyone else's vision for how the trip should go. According to healthadvocate.com, if you're sitting down with friends or family to discuss your upcoming getaway, there are a few things you'll want to consider:

- Discuss everyone's expectations for the trip.
- List activities, sights, and other places everyone is interested in. If you're traveling with kids and teenagers, allow them to choose from activities they may enjoy doing so they feel included.
- Prioritize the list so the "must-dos" are completed, and no one misses out on an experience they were really looking forward to.
- Acknowledge before you go that not everyone will get to do everything they want to do at all times.
- Agree to compromise. Compromising is one of the most critical parts of a successful family vacation. If everyone gets some of what they want, everyone will be much happier.

After this, think about past family trips, and at what points things could have been better. Consider the following questions:

- What went wrong?
- Where, when, and how did things start to go bad?
- What actions can you take to avoid or resolve these issues if they present themselves during this vacation?

Do your best to make the intel briefing fun and engaging. No one wants to sit in the living room and listen to you drone on about crime statistics, so have some fun facts available about some of the things you'll be seeing and doing. I also find that it's a good idea to have a few surprises up your sleeve to get everyone excited about the upcoming trip. "Guess what, kids? If you behave and listen, we're also going to visit the world's largest ice cream store!" (That's a real thing. It's called The Ice Cream Farm, and it's in Chester, UK.) In the end, you're using this time to express your security concerns, and you want those to be taken seriously, but at the same time, you want the group to get excited about what's to come, so make sure you're striking the proper balance during the intelligence briefing.

Key Points:

- If you found information relevant to the group's safety during your intelligence gathering, share it during the intel briefing.
- It's imperative everyone understand what areas you'll be visiting, what the likelihood of danger will be, and in what regions frequent communication and sticking together will be critical.
- Aside from the obvious safety concerns, the intel briefing is also a great time to consider the rest of the group's wants, needs, and opinions.

5

Equipment Check

AFTER THE INTEL BRIEFING, equipment checks are a vital part of your travel preparations. Nothing is more annoying than getting to your hotel room, unpacking, and realizing that you forgot your phone charger, or getting home from a trip and realizing you left your favorite jacket hanging in the hotel room closet. Although these issues aren't exactly life-threatening, they can be incredibly frustrating. Forgetting to pack your toothbrush may seem like a minor annoyance, but if you're anything like me, it can distract you to the point that you lose focus on the more important things, like properly securing your room. (More on that later.) The good news is that these inconveniences can be avoided by staying organized and planning ahead. I've found that the best way to keep things in order is to make a list. I always break my packing lists down into several main categories, such as:

- Clothing
- Travel documents
- Medications
- Toiletries
- Travel tech (cellphones, laptops, headphones, chargers)
- Miscellaneous

Then I fill those in with specific items as I pack. What ends up in the suitcase will always depend on the length and purpose of the trip. I'm sure everyone reading this has at some point packed a bag, and everyone has their own system, so I'm not going to focus on details, but I will point out that equipment checks should happen at several specific points during your trip.

1. Before leaving the house
2. Before getting off an airplane
3. Before leaving your room, if you're headed out to explore
4. Before checking out of your hotel room and returning home
5. Any time you take things out of your bag
6. Once you return home

Be sure to make a list for each bag you pack. If you're flying, you may have a checked bag as well as a carry-on. Place a list in with each individual bag so you know exactly what should be in it. It's also a good idea to make a copy of each list and keep it with your travel documents. Those copies will come in handy if a bag is ever lost or stolen.

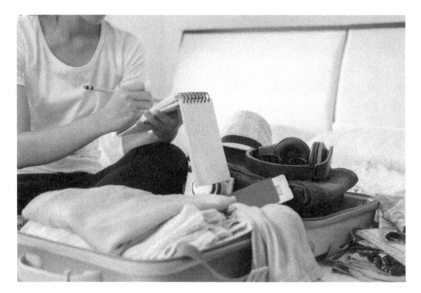

Equipment checks are simply a way of keeping your personal items in order and making sure you have everything you need. They're essential to your safety because finding yourself on a train in Europe miles away from your hotel and realizing you forgot your child's inhaler could be disastrous. Now let's take a step back and cover a few things that may not automatically come to mind when you're packing for your next trip.

Aside from the standard toiletries and clothing items I need for a trip, I also pack a few things that aren't so standard. Some people may find these items odd, but there are five things that I never check into a hotel without.

1. **Three rubber door wedges:** You can pick up door wedges at any hardware store for a couple of bucks. They're lightweight and packable so they won't be a hassle to get from point A to point B. Once you get into your lodgings, place a wedge underneath each entry point before you go to bed. Typical hotel room locks are easy to bypass, but these rubber wedges will slow down any intruder who may try to enter your room, and allow you precious seconds to call the police or notify security.

2. **A roll of clear Scotch tape:** Scotch tape is a very useful item, and when applied correctly can help ensure your security by alerting you to any tampering that may occur while you're out. If you pack items away in drawers or cabinets inside your hotel room, place a small piece of clear tape at the corner of the drawer or door. You can also protect the main entrance to your room this way. Once you've left, place a small piece of clear Scotch tape along the bottom of the door and attach it to the frame in a manner that will dislodge it if the door is opened. Small pieces of clear tape are almost invisible to anyone who doesn't know they are there and will let you know if someone has entered your room or tampered with anything while you were out.

3. **Portable motion alarms:** Small battery-operated motion alarms are a great idea if you plan on visiting unfamiliar territory. These small, packable alarms are affordable and can be used inside your lodgings at night as an extra layer of security. Most alarms also come with a manual activation switch that triggers the audible alarm and can be used to draw attention to your situation and dissuade any would be attackers. This comes in handy if you're outside your room and mobile.

4. **Portable fireproof money bag:** This one may not be something you automatically think of when you're packing, but they're indispensable if you're traveling with large amounts of cash or any valuables. Most hotel room safes are cheap and don't have a very good fire safety rating. But if you place your money or valuables in a fireproof bag before putting them in the safe, you're increasing the chances they won't be destroyed in the event of a fire.

5. **International electrical adapter and portable phone charger:** This is if I'm traveling internationally; more on this in chapter ten.

You may find other items and gadgets that can help with security related issues, but these are the five I've found indispensable. You can pick up all five for under fifty dollars, which is a small price to pay for a little extra piece of mind.

Now that the bags are packed, it's time to hit the road. This is an exciting moment, but now's not the time to let your guard down and forget about security. There are still plenty of things you need to consider, so let's take a look at some of the last-minute mistakes people tend to make that can open them up to attacks at home.

Key Points:

- Equipment checks are a vital part of your travel preparations.
- Break your packing lists down into several main categories, such as:

  - Clothing
  - Travel documents
  - Medications
  - Toiletries
  - Travel tech (cellphones, laptops, headphones, chargers)
  - Miscellaneous

- Equipment checks should happen at several specific points during your trip.

  - Before leaving the house
  - Before getting off an airplane
  - Before leaving your room if you're headed out to explore
  - Before checking out of your hotel room and returning home
  - Any time you take things out of your bag

- Place a list in with each individual bag so you know exactly what should be in it.
- Aside from the standard toiletries and clothing items, you should also pack the following:

  - Three rubber door wedges
  - A roll of clear Scotch tape
  - Portable motion alarms
  - Portable fireproof money bag
  - International electrical adapter and portable phone charger

6

Things to Avoid

AT THIS POINT, you've picked your vacation destination, determined your mode of travel, set up accommodations, conducted a thorough threat assessment, and recruited a solid support team to help secure your home. Things are shaping up nicely, so it's easy to get excited about sharing your plans with others. There's no issue with wanting to talk to others about your upcoming getaway, but there are definitely a few pitfalls you may want to avoid. In a significant number of cases, the biggest of these pitfalls is social media.

I call this book series the Spotting Danger series for a reason. According to Rescue Time, a screen time monitoring software company, Americans generally spend three hours and fifteen minutes a day looking at their smartphones. A large majority of that time is spent on social media outlets such as Facebook and Instagram. Social media is a fantastic way to share your experiences with friends and family and keep tabs on the people you're closest to, but it shouldn't draw your attention away from your surroundings to the point that you're endangering your safety. I personally use social media extensively to promote my business and keep in touch with family and old army buddies, but there are also some downsides to the use of social media, especially when planning a getaway. Here are a few Facebook statistics to help put things in perspective:

- Worldwide, there are over 2.45 billion monthly active users (MAU) as of September 2019. (Source: Facebook 10/30/19)
- On average, 1.62 billion people log onto Facebook daily and are considered daily active users (Facebook DAU). This stat tends to fluctuate but has steadily increased since 2019.
- The most common age demographic is age twenty-five to thirty-four.
- Five new profiles are created every second.
- There are 83 million fake profiles. (Source: CNN)

That last point should be an eye-opener. You may think that posting your plans on Facebook or Instagram is harmless and wouldn't draw any attention from strangers, but there is a staggering number of people on those platforms, some of whom are there surfing for targets of opportunity. According to a study conducted by the home security company ADT, 78 percent of burglars use Facebook and Twitter to target personal properties.[5]

Not all burglars are bumbling idiots straight out of the *Home Alone* movies. Some are very sophisticated and use social media to target and track potential victims. If you "check in" at a movie theatre or a restaurant, criminals who are watching can assume you'll be away from home for at least a few hours, giving them plenty of time for a quick smash and grab. When you post your vacation pictures, they know they may have several days to plan their attack. Even casual mentions of weekend plans or upcoming social events can open up windows of opportunity and leave your home vulnerable to burglars. Given these facts, there are a few preventive measures you can take to make sure you're not oversharing on social media.

---

5. https://www.adt.co.uk/blog/adts-top-tips-for-online-security.

- **Privacy settings:** Tighten up your privacy settings to better control who can see your social media posts.
- **Friend requests:** Never accept a friend request from people you do not know. This could very possibly be a criminal looking for potential targets.
- **Checking in:** Don't "check in" on social media when you're out to the movies, dinner, or any other place where people can assume you'll be away from home for several hours.
- **Posts about routines:** Avoid sharing information about your daily routines. Information such as commute times, gym schedules, and weekend getaways can leave you open to targeting.
- **Vacation plans:** Never share details about upcoming travel plans. Photos from your vacation should be closely held and shared on social media only after you've made it safely home.
- **Location settings:** Always turn off your social media location features. These can automatically tag any photos you post and give away your whereabouts.

Aside from the pitfalls of social media, it's easy to overshare information in general when you're planning your vacation. Be careful not to discuss travel plans when you're at the grocery store checkout counter, barbershop, or other public places where people may overhear you. I worked for years as a correctional officer in the federal prison system and was amazed at how many criminals said they picked their targets simply by keeping their ears open and listening to the people around them. We're social creatures by nature, and some of us are prone to talking too much when it comes to sharing details about our lives. Always be alert to the people around you.

Now that your planning stages are completed, you should feel pretty good about beginning your vacation. Thanks to the preparations you've made, your home now gives the appearance of a hard target and will be much less appealing to potential criminals. It's now time to relinquish control to your support system and start focusing on the travel phase of your getaway. This is where you need to shift gears and get your head up. Now that it's time to hit the road, your situational awareness will be front and center when it comes to your personal safety. The following chapters will review some of the concepts covered in my first book *Spotting Danger Before It Spots You* and serve as a refresher about the basics of situational awareness. I will go a step further in the next section and cover how situational awareness works across multiple modes of travel. Some of the things you need to be aware of when you're driving may be much different than the circumstances you find yourself in while flying. Although the mode of travel may change, the importance of situational awareness during this phase of your vacation cannot be overstated. So let's get started.

Key Points:

- According to a study conducted by the home security company ADT, 78 percent of burglars use Facebook and Twitter to target personal properties.
- If you "check in" at a movie theatre or a restaurant, criminals who are watching can assume that you'll be away from home for at least a few hours.
- Preventive measures you can take to make sure you're not over-sharing on social media:

  o Privacy settings: Tighten up your privacy settings to better control who can see your social media posts.
  o Friend requests: Never accept a friend request from people you do not know.
  o Checking in: Don't "check in" on social media when you're out to the movies, dinner, or any other location where people can assume you'll be away from home for several hours.
  o Posts about routines: Avoid sharing information about your daily routines.

○ Vacation plans: Never share details about upcoming travel plans. Photos from your vacation should be closely held and shared on social media only after you've made it safely home.

○ Location settings: Always turn off your social media location features. These can automatically tag any photos you post and give away your whereabouts.

• Be careful not to discuss travel plans when you're at the grocery store checkout counter, barbershop, or other public places where people may overhear you.

PHASE TWO—Travel

"Strong and content I travel the open road."
—WALT WHITMAN

7

Getting "Switched On"——The Basics of Situational Awareness

NOW LET'S GET BACK to the basics of personal safety. Believe it or not, in the vast majority of cases, when someone intends to do you harm, they will inadvertently telegraph their intentions through something known as pre-incident indicators. These pre-incident indicators are sometimes subtle, sometimes overt, but consistently observable if you know what to look for. I liken this process to boxing. If you've ever seen a professional fight, you've witnessed this scenario before. One boxer will pin the other against the ropes and unleash a flurry of punches—jabs, crosses, hooks, and uppercuts—all seemingly knock-out punches, but not one of them lands on their intended target. The other boxer casually slips and dodges every punch. Then he maneuvers himself back to the center of the ring unscathed, ready for the counterattack. When you view this process in real-time, it looks almost superhuman, but the hard-to-hit boxer doesn't possess any special powers; he's simply looking for his opponent to telegraph their intentions so he can avoid the punches. If he's studied his opponent closely enough, he'll know that his right shoulder dips just before throwing a hook or that he drops his hip as he's setting up for the uppercut. These small movements are the pre-incident indicators, and knowing how to interpret them is what wins fights. By studying these actions and learning what they mean, boxers give themselves an advantage and can effectively counter an attack before it's ever launched. That's not a superpower; it's just good situational awareness.

This same concept is what you're about to learn. Before leaving home, you need to understand who your opponent is and how they work. You will learn what pre-incident indicators predatorial criminals tend to adhere to and what those indicators mean. This, in turn, will better prepare you to identify potential problems and avoid violent attacks before they ever have a chance to materialize.

When I worked as a federal air marshal, this process of tuning in to your environment and looking for pre-incident indicators was known as being "switched on." Being switched on was critical to our success because the most dangerous enemies are those who have become comfortable with violence. The more practiced the attack, the smoother they become, and the less likely it will be that their victims ever see it coming. That's why situational awareness is so important. Without it, those pre-incident indicators become much harder to spot. Victims are caught off guard, and when everything is said and done, you'll often hear them say things like, "He came out of nowhere," or, "I never saw it coming." I don't want that to be you!

This phase of the book will cover the basics of situational awareness and give you the tools you need to correctly identify those actions that are precursors to violence. More importantly, this section will teach you ways to interact with your environment that make you much less appealing to predatory criminals. A few of the things we'll cover here are:

- How your body language signals either vulnerability or strength
- How to read your environment and what to do with the information you're collecting

- What specific actions you should be looking for, and what they mean to your safety
- How to spot potential security risks within your environment
- What steps to take once a threat has materialized

These are a pretty handy set of skills to have, and they don't require that you be a black belt in jiu-jitsu or carry a gun. Those things definitely harden your personal defenses, but without situational awareness, they're just window dressing. As I often say, "You can't fight what you don't see coming." What you're about to learn is the cornerstone of any good self-defense program. Plus, by learning to be more in tune with your environment and less focused on minor distractions, your next vacation will be all the more enjoyable. So, with that being said, let's get switched on.

7.1 Don't Be a Target

There are a lot of factors at play when it comes to how predatory criminals select their victims. What I find interesting is that criminals tend to stick with a specific set of rules when picking their targets, and those rules remain consistent no matter where in the world you may find yourself. People who make their living victimizing others have this process of selection down to a science.

Before we get into the method itself, let's take a closer look at the types of predatory criminals and what drives them to violence in the first place. Predators can generally be broken down into two basic groups: resource predators and process predators. A resource predator is looking for tangible items, be it cash, jewelry, or even your clothing. They've decided they need something and that they're going to take it from you. Predators in this category include your basic mugger, pickpocket, or burglar. In some cases, if a resource predator confronts you and you just give them what they want, they go away. The process predator, on the other hand, is much different. The process predator isn't interested in your watch or wallet; they get off on the act of violence itself. This category of predator includes the likes of rapists and murderers. Although their motivations may differ, the process that these two types of criminals use to select their victims stays consistent.

In my first book *Spotting Danger Before It Spots You*, I cover how criminals tend to label their victims as either hard targets or soft targets and how those two categories can apply to both people and places. For instance, people can be considered hard targets when they appear aware of their surroundings, carry themselves with confidence, and look like they could handle themselves in a fight. Much like a bank, they are displaying visible defenses against an attack.

Conversely, places that are considered soft targets have no visible signs of security. There are no locks, cameras, or fences, and admittance is open to everyone. People are considered soft targets when they display none of the outward signs of awareness or preparation. They look easy to approach and ill-prepared to defend themselves should they be confronted with violence. Predators prefer soft targets because they pose little or no threat to their own well-being. Criminals carefully measure risk versus reward and will almost always take the easier path. This process of elimination and target selection can be completed in as little as seven seconds. In that short span of time, a predator can accurately determine the following:

1. Their initial perception of how you will react during a violent encounter
2. The amount of risk you pose to them
3. The amount of observable value you possess
4. Your visible defenses

These four factors, Perception, Risk, Observable Value, and Defenses, are what I refer to as the PROD. It's critical that you become familiar with these elements of selection because when it comes to a violent encounter, they answer the question, "Why me?" Now let's take a closer look at each element of the PROD.

Perception

How do you think other people view you? Do you come across as outgoing and independent, or are you more introverted and shy? How others perceive us has everything to do with the way we are treated, and it is a key element in how criminals select their victims. In 1981, a study conducted by sociologists Betty Grayson and Morris Stein found that a significant consideration in target selection was body language. They identified basic movements that were signs of weakness:

- Short, shuffling strides when walking
- Not swinging the arms in proportion with the stride
- Exaggerated side-to-side movement when walking
- Head facing at a downward angle when walking

On the other hand, the study also revealed specific movements that indicated the target would be harder to approach and, therefore, not likely to be selected as a victim. These included:

- Medium to long stride when walking
- Arms swinging in proportion to their stride
- Body movement in vertical alignment, which was viewed as a strong and determined walking pattern
- Head level and eyes visible when walking

We may view ourselves one way but be seen entirely differently by others based solely on our movements. Since you now know what physical actions signal vulnerability, you can take significant steps toward protecting yourself simply by modifying your body language. Just changing your posture and stride can make you look more like someone who would be difficult to subdue and who would likely put up a fight if attacked—in other words, a hard target.

Risk

Predators go through the process of target selection and attack planning to ensure their success while minimizing risk to themselves. If they feel they can confront you with minimal danger, they are more likely to act. When measuring risk, criminals look for simple things: Are you with a group of friends? Do you look like the type of person who would fight back or cause a scene? Are you alert and moving with a purpose, or are you distracted? Some signals are more subtle; someone who frequently avoids eye contact, for instance, would be viewed as timid and therefore pose little or no risk to the attacker. That may seem inconsequential to you, but to a criminal, it could be the deciding factor.

Risk or even the perception of risk is something most predators will go out of their way to avoid, so take a look at your current situation. What attributes do you possess that would pose a risk to predators? What things could you change to decrease the chance of an unwanted approach? Sometimes, little things can make a big difference. When you're out and about, just keeping your head up and looking around makes you look more imposing. Walking with a dog is a fantastic deterrent. Traveling with a group or in well-lit areas definitely decreases the likelihood you'll be targeted. The bottom line is this: anything you can do to increase the risk you pose to a predator will be worth the effort.

Observable Value

When you think of value, what comes to mind? A big house, a nice car, expensive jewelry? We all have an image in our mind of what value looks like, but value is subjective and can look much different to you than it does to a potential attacker. I'm not telling you what to wear out at night or what jewelry is most appropriate in public, but I will tell you that if you have anything of value on your person that's visible to others, it's a good idea to display more outward signs of security by moving with purpose, minimizing your distractions, and staying alert to your surroundings.

Defenses

Imagine for a moment that you're a burglar casing two houses in a nice neighborhood. Both houses have well-manicured yards and give the impression that someone wealthy lives inside. You know you can find something of value in either place; the only question is which one to break into. One of the first things you may do as a criminal is walk up to the house and ring the doorbell to make sure no one is at home. Let's say when you approach the first house you notice home security stickers on the front windows and door, and the doorbell has a monitored security camera attached to it. You know right away you're being watched. When you ring the doorbell, you hear a huge dog barking on the other side of the entrance. Now a voice comes over an external intercom asking who you are and what you want. Seeing these visible defenses in action, you know that whatever value may lie inside those walls isn't worth the risk to your personal safety, so you move on. There are no security stickers at the next house, and the doorbell is broken, so you knock; no dog is barking inside, so you move around to the back door. There are no signs of security, and the rear of the house isn't visible to any of the neighbors. You've found your target. The risk to you is minimal, and whatever you may find inside will be of some value, so you break the lock and go to work. This same concept applies to every person walking down the street. If someone is set on taking something from you, the first thing they will do is evaluate your visible defenses and decide whether or not you have something of value or if you pose a threat to their personal safety. Regardless of the level of value you may possess, your defenses are what will serve as the deterrent to attack.

By thoroughly understanding the PROD method of target selection, you're giving yourself some valuable insight into how and why predators choose their targets. This little bit of knowledge goes a long way in helping to develop your situational awareness, but there's a lot more to consider. Now let's take a look at some other factors that directly impact your safety when traveling.

7.2 Understand Your Surroundings

What does situational awareness look like to you? Is it a man sitting in a dark corner with his back to the wall, staring doggedly at every person who walks through the door, constantly scanning for signs of danger? That sounds more like a scene from a bad gangster movie. Real situational awareness isn't about staying so tightly wound that you stress yourself out. In fact, when implemented correctly, situational awareness can allow you to relax more and enjoy yourself without the stress of thinking there's a threat around every corner. But before you can do that, you're going to need some information up front.

Situational awareness requires that you have a good understanding of your environment, how people dress and act, the general mood of a place, and a basic knowledge of the local customs. Some of this information you've already gathered during your threat assessment, but most of what you'll be applying is just good old-fashioned common sense. For instance, if you're headed off to the beach, you know before you get there how most people will behave, how they'll be dressed, and what activities you'll see them engaged in. You know all these things in advance because you understand what a day on the beach is like. That generalized knowledge of acceptable behaviors within your environment is known as a baseline. Even if you're unfamiliar with a particular setting, it only takes a moment to settle in and get a sense of what's happening around you. Here's an example.

Let's say you're invited to a get-together at a friend's house. You have little or no knowledge of what kind of event you'll be attending, but you do know that this particular friend is mostly quiet and reserved, so you dress casually, grab a nice bottle of wine, and head on over. You expect to be greeted at the door, thanked for the gift, and invited in for dinner and some casual conversation. Seems reasonable, right? But once you get there, you realize this isn't that kind of get-to-gether at all. It's a complete stranger who throws open the door, music is blasting from the front room, and there are people everywhere dancing, drinking, and having a good time. The shock of walking into something unexpected may take some getting used to, but once you're inside, it only takes a few seconds for you to look around, settle into your new environment, and establish that baseline of behavior. There's nothing complicated about understanding how people should act in that situation. It's only when someone acts outside the established baseline that you need to pay closer attention and start looking for problems that could affect your safety. So, let's take a look at how that process plays out in real life.

Readers of my first book, *Spotting Danger Before It Spots You*, will remember the story of Ahmed Ressam. I repeat it here because it perfectly illustrates how situational awareness can not only make people safer but also save lives. On December 14, 1999, a twenty-three-year-old man named Ahmed Ressam packed his rented Chrysler sedan with explosives and drove onto the ferry from Victoria, Canada, to Port Angeles, Washington. After clearing customs, Ressam planned on driving to Los Angeles where he would detonate a massive bomb outside the LAX airport on New Year's Day. At the Immigration and Naturalization Service inspection station in Victoria, Ressam presented agents with his Canadian passport. He had torn the Afghanistan entry and exit stamps from his passport to avoid suspicion. The INS agent on duty ran the passport through various databases and allowed Ressam to board the ferry. Later that day, Ressam arrived in Port Angeles in Washington State. He waited for all the other cars to depart the ferry, assuming that the last vehicle off would draw less scrutiny.

Alert customs officers assigned to the port began to notice that Ressam's behaviors didn't seem quite right. Despite the freezing temperatures, he drove with his window down, and he compulsively cleared his throat due to his prior exposure to the caustic chemicals used in making the explosives. He appeared to be overly nervous; he paced the dock of the ferry and was sweating profusely. These agents under-stood the baseline behaviors of the passengers that frequented the ferry, and Ressam's actions fell way outside of that baseline, so they quickly referred him to secondary inspection. When asked for addi-tional identification, Ressam handed the customs agent a Costco membership card. As that agent began an initial pat-search, Ressam panicked and tried to run away but was quickly apprehended. Inspec-tors examining Ressam's rental car later found the explosives con-cealed in the spare tire well, but at first, they assumed the white powder and gelatinous liquid were drug related until an inspector pried apart and identified one of the four timing devices concealed inside a black box. Ressam was placed under arrest, and thousands of lives were potentially saved due to the quick observations of the agents.

Whether it's a terrorist like Ressam or a common street thug, those who wish to harm others typically go through the process of target selection and attack planning. Ahmed Ressam carefully planned his attack and chose his target based on the number of potential casual-ties a massive explosion would produce and the amount of media cov-erage it would receive. During the planning stages, Ressam chose what he felt was a "soft target" for his point of entry. He picked Port Ange-les based on its daily traffic and the limited number of staff working the port. He knew that if he timed his entry just right, the agents working the port would be nearing the end of their shift and would be more likely to overlook something during their inspections. What Res-sam didn't account for during his risk versus reward assessment was the devastating effect one alert agent would have on his well-laid plans.

That's why situational awareness is so important. Inevitably, a crim-inal will somehow reveal themselves through their actions at some point during the process of target selection. These actions can only be observed and interpreted by those who are paying attention to what's happening around them and understand the established baseline. Now let's look at how actions that fall outside that baseline affect your safety and what steps you should take once they're encountered.

7.3 Identify Problems

Once you've become accustomed to your surroundings, it's time to start looking for actions that fall outside of what is considered normal behavior. These actions are referred to as baseline anomalies, and there's a process to their identification. This first step is known as the initial scan. Any time you enter into a new space, be it a room, a parking lot, or a public event, you need to begin an analysis of your surroundings. This is extremely important when you're traveling, because virtually everywhere you go is "a new space." At this point, you're not going to be staring everyone down and sizing them up for a potential fight; all you're doing now is asking yourself one question: "Does this place have a positive feeling or a negative feeling?" Some of what you feel will be based on intuition, and we'll cover that in more detail later. A few seconds of your time and a quick glance around can give you the first bit of information you need to determine whether or not an area, a person, or a situation is playing by the rules of the baseline.

Suppose the general feeling you get after your initial scan is a negative one. In that case, you have two options: leave the area immediately or start taking a closer look at your surroundings to gather more detailed information. What exactly aroused your suspicion and drew your focus? Was it a specific person or an event within your environment that seemed outside the norm? Or was there a general shift in mood or attitude among a particular group? This is where we begin the second step in the process, the detailed scan.

During the detailed scan, you recognize and collect behavioral cues that help you identify people within your area who may be up to no good. For instance, imagine you're vacationing with a few friends, and you're about to attend a pool party. You've been to this area before, so you know the layout and the general mood among this particular group of friends. When you walk into the pool area, your initial scan reveals that all is as it should be—the mood is upbeat, the music is loud, and people are wearing the appropriate pool attire. You feel comfortable in these surroundings, and everything seems to be well within the baseline. At this point, it's okay to relax and maintain a casual state of awareness while you continue to monitor your surroundings. Now imagine that someone enters the pool area from a side entrance; you don't immediately recognize this person, and they're not dressed appropriately for the occasion. Instead of being relaxed and ready to party, this person seems tense and agitated. His hands are shoved deep into his pockets, and he's staring intently at one particular group near the pool. These actions fall well outside of your established baseline, so now it's time to begin your detailed scan.

During the detailed scan you're looking for actions that indicate signs of potential violence. These actions are known as pre-incident indicators and they include the following:

- **Hidden hands:** The hands are what can kill you. Someone who is hiding their hands may also be concealing their intent to harm you.
- **Inexplicable presence:** Does the person who caught your attention have a reason for being where they are? Is their presence justified and their actions in alignment with the baseline behaviors of that area?
- **Target glancing:** Predators like to keep an eye on their prey, but in an attempt to avoid eye contact, they will continually glance at and away from their intended victim.
- **A sudden change of movement:** If you feel that you are being followed and suddenly change your direction of travel, keep an eye on the people around you. If someone inexplicably changes their direction of travel to match yours, you could be their target.
- **Inappropriate clothing:** Like the man who just entered the pool area, someone who is wearing more clothing than is appropriate may be trying to hide something.

- **Seeking a position of advantage:** Predators like to keep the upper hand. In an attempt to gain dominance, they will try to maneuver themselves into positions where they know they will have the tactical advantage. For example, an aggressor may try to back you into a corner where escape would be more difficult, or purposely block an exit.

- **Impeding your movement:** If someone inexplicably blocks your movement in a particular direction, there's a pretty good chance they're trying to funnel you into a position of disadvantage.

- **Unsolicited attempts at conversation:** If someone you are unfamiliar with approaches you and makes an attempt at unsolicited small talk, take a very close look at your situation. Are you in a position of disadvantage? Are there other people in the area? Has this person shown other pre-incident indicators that lead you to believe they have bad intentions? Attempts at small talk are often the predator's last move before the attack.

Aside from the pre-incident indicators we just covered, there are also specific uncontrollable physiological reactions to stress that act as precursors to violent action. These are important to note because they hold true across all cultures, races, genders, and age groups, which is pretty handy when you're traveling through unfamiliar territory. Here are a few of the more common physiological indicators.

- **Heavier-than usual-breathing:** When someone is under stress, his or her respiratory system is immediately affected. They begin to breathe more heavily or take sudden deep breaths to help distribute oxygen-rich blood to their extremities just in case they feel the need to fight or flee. Someone who intends to assault another person may appear to be breathing heavier than normal as they "psych themselves up" for the attack.

- **Appearing tense:** When we're placed under stress, our muscles naturally tense up to help protect us from injury and pain.

- **Posturing:** Frequently, people who feel threatened will naturally attempt to make themselves appear bigger. They'll puff out their chest, spread their arms, or become louder to ward off any potential threats or intimidate their intended victims.
- **Pupil dilation:** This is when a person's pupils appear larger and is often associated with fear and anger. Usually, a person's pupils are two to five millimeters in diameter, but they can dilate to as large as nine millimeters when they feel threatened. This can take place within the space of a second and is a sure-fire way to gauge a person's emotional state—but it also requires you to be dangerously close to the subject.
- **Excessive sweating:** Sweating is a natural reaction to fear and stress regardless of the outside temperature.

These five items are not all-inclusive, but they offer a pretty good sample of normal physiological reactions to stressful circumstances. When paired with the known pre-incident indicators, they can quickly help identify someone who may be up to no good.

Monitoring the Baseline

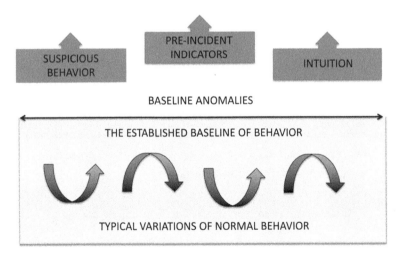

Now let's revisit our suspicious visitor at the pool. During your detailed scan, you make note of a few critical factors. The man is dressed inappropriately for the occasion, he's displaying signs of tension and nervousness, and he's hiding his hands. These actions raise your suspicion to the level that you feel your safety could be in jeopardy, so now what? As you start devising a plan to get yourself and your friends to safety, you notice the man smile warmly at someone near the edge of the pool. They acknowledge each other, and the person by the pool waves the stranger over. They shake hands and start talking. The stranger is then introduced to the rest of the group, and someone hands him a drink. These actions bring the situation back down to the normal baseline of behaviors, so you relax and continue to enjoy yourself while casually monitoring your surroundings.

Now that you see how this process of observation works, let's talk for a moment about intuition and how it impacts your awareness and safety. What if you walk into a room and instantly get a negative feeling about the people around you or the area in general? You don't notice anything that falls outside the baseline, but you have that "gut feeling" that something is wrong. What should you do? Your actions will vary depending on the situation, and we'll focus more on that later. But for now, let's discuss the role of intuition, what it is, what it means, and how it could possibly save your life.

One of nature's most extraordinary achievements is the human brain, and it works most efficiently when it feels that its host is in danger. What most people refer to as intuition is actually a cognitive process, and when we feel threatened, our minds often move faster than we can control or perceive. We sometimes second-guess our gut feelings because we put much more faith in the logical step-by-step approach to thinking. Some of the signals our brain sends us to warn of danger we disregard as trivial and unimportant because it's too hard for us to cognitively connect the dots between what we see and the risk that lies ahead. We owe it to ourselves to pay closer attention to what we refer to as "bad feelings." There's science behind your body's natural reactions to fear, even if you haven't consciously registered the fact that you're afraid. Fear stimulates your brain and triggers a release of adrenaline and other stress hormones throughout your body. This rush of adrenaline is what causes your heart to race and your palms to sweat. It's also responsible for goosebumps, which are what make your hair stand on end. Goosebumps are the result of a reflex that causes the muscles attached to the base of each hair follicle to contract; these contractions force the hairs outward and make them feel as if they're "standing up." The adrenaline rush also causes the blood to move from your limbs and into your core to protect the vital organs and fuel larger muscle groups for the fight to come. This creates a tingling feeling in your extremities that most people refer to as "the chills."

We often experience these subtle signals but don't recognize them for what they are. Our brains have taken in information that it quickly registered as a threat and passed that information directly to our adrenal glands, completely bypassing what we consider to be rational thought. It's often well after an attack that a victim can look back and remember with some level of clarity what it was that actually alerted them to danger.

A basic understanding of situational awareness, predatory behaviors, and pre-incident indicators can absolutely save your life, but the importance of recognizing and properly interpreting intuitive thought cannot be overstated. It's your brain's way of bypassing the sometimes slow and cumbersome process of logical thinking and warning you that something is wrong. We humans are the only animals on the planet that will look a predator right in the face, and instead of immediately retreating, try to rationalize its presence. This lack of trust in intuition can cause hesitation when action is required and very possibly jeopardize your safety. Always listen to your intuition.

7.4 Anticipate Outcomes

Up to this point, you've learned how to read your surroundings and developed the ability to differentiate between normal and abnormal behaviors within your environment. You've also discovered how variations in those behaviors could impact your safety and how they stay consistent no matter where your travels may take you. Now let's dive into how you can develop plans for avoidance or escape based on the information your environment is providing.

Anytime you're confronted by violence, there are decisions to be made—decisions that may well have a lasting impact on how you live the rest of your life. Regardless of the motivating factors behind crime, the end result is always the same for the victim. The shock, emotional trauma, and physical damage suffered during an act of violence can resonate with victims for years. That raises the question: What's the best way to keep yourself safe? What options do you have? When it comes to a violent encounter, you have four alternatives: avoidance, escape, de-escalation, and confrontation. These four options are universal and remain consistent no matter where your travels may take you. Let's take a closer look at each; then, we'll discuss how these options factor into your decision-making.

Avoidance: The nature of self-defense is subjective. There is no one best way to defend yourself against an attacker, but in most cases, if danger is spotted early and there is a reasonable avenue for avoidance, removing yourself from the situation gives you your best chance at survival. Even in the absence of obvious danger, there are several avoidance tactics you can use while traveling that go a long way in keeping yourself safe.

- Stay away from places you know to be high-crime areas or frequented by dangerous people.
- Always be aware of your surroundings.

- Make yourself a hard target, or at least try not to look like a soft target.
- Do not provoke people or allow verbal conflicts to escalate.

One essential element of avoidance is distance. Situational awareness allows you to increase the range at which you see potential problems coming. The further off you can spot a dangerous situation, the more time you have to remove yourself from the equation. No victim, no crime.

Escape: If complete avoidance of a situation is impossible, distance also removes the attacker's opportunity to do harm. If you're in an area you consider safe and you're surrounded by people you know to be friends, there's little need to concern yourself with personal space. If, however, you're in an unfamiliar setting populated by strangers, then maintaining a safe distance is prudent and can give you valuable time to spot and react to potential danger. Aside from keeping safe distances, several other options need to be considered when making an escape.

- Are there entrances and exits available to you that can aid in your escape?
- In the absence of a viable exit, is there anywhere to hide?
- Is there anything you can use to divert the attacker's attention from you?
- Is there any way to create an obstacle between you and the attacker?
- Were there any safe spaces you spotted along your route that you could retreat to?
- Are there any items nearby you could use against the attacker to create space?

These are just a few possibilities when it comes to making a getaway. Always remember that there is no substitute for sound awareness and planning.

De-escalation: In the absence of an escape route, de-escalation is the next best option. The quickest way to de-escalate a bad situation is just to give the attacker what they want, but keep in mind that this only works with a resource predator (someone who is using you to get something). There's no guarantee that handing over your valuables will stop that person from causing you harm, but it will increase your odds of escaping safely. It's a risk that you will have to weigh and act upon in the moment. The other option for de-escalation is through communication, but this can devolve quickly due to the overcharged emotional states accompanying confrontation. Some keys to effective communication are:

- Speak calmly but with confidence. Confidence is key here. Never let yourself appear timid when engaging a potential attacker in conversation.
- Try to keep a safe distance, but stay close enough to build rapport or react if things turn bad—just out of hand's reach is a good rule to follow.
- Don't act scared. Acting scared or timid will only encourage an attacker and escalate the situation.
- Don't try to be intimidating. Trying to be overly intimidating toward potential attackers will only inflame their egos and escalate the situation.
- Watch body language. Look for changes in posture and levels of aggression. Subtle changes in body language such as balling up fists or slightly turning their feet to get into a "fighting stance" are good indicators that an attack is coming.
- Empathize—show some level of understanding of the attacker's situation. You may have to fake this part, but do it if it allows you or your family a safe means of escape.

- Allow the attacker a way out. Never corner someone when you're trying to de-escalate a situation. Allowing the other person a way out gives them an option other than fighting.

When it comes to using effective communication to de-escalate a heated argument, keep in mind that not everyone speaks your language. If you find yourself overseas and confronted with both an attacker and a language barrier, keep your hands open and up in a defensive position. Speak calmly and monitor the situation for changes. Regardless of what language is being spoken, remembering these techniques will be your best bet at survival.

Confrontation: In the unfortunate event that avoidance is impossible, communication breaks down, and de-escalation is no longer an option, confrontation may be the only solution to the problem. This is a scary realization for a lot of people. That's why I recommend seeking out competent instruction in some form of self-defense. There is no one best way to defend yourself in a fight, but whatever approach you choose to take, take it wholeheartedly. When it comes to confrontation, speed, surprise, and aggression are the keys to survival. Once you've been backed into a corner and left with no visible means of escape, there's no point in waiting for the aggressor to attack. Fight like your life depends on it. Once you've created enough space to disengage, do so, then remove yourself from the situation and alert law enforcement as quickly as possible.

Now that you have a pretty good understanding of what options are available to you, how do you go about choosing the one that gives you the outcome you're looking for? The answer to that question will depend on your level of situational awareness and how quickly you can respond once a violent situation presents itself. The amount of time you have to react will be dependent on your ability to anticipate the actions of other people. This skill set can be developed through what I call "what-if games."

What-if games are an extremely effective way to increase situational awareness and decrease reaction times in a violent encounter, especially when you're in unfamiliar surroundings. These games can be played in any environment and are most effective when played with others. Here's how it's done. Whenever you're out and about, whether on vacation, picking the kids up from school, or out to dinner with the family, take note of your position within your environment and ask yourself questions about how you would react in certain situations. Start simply and then build on the scenario. You are only limited by your imagination. Here's an example.

The next time you're out to dinner with your friends or family think about this: what if someone enters through the back of the restaurant with a gun and begins shooting randomly? Ask yourself the following questions and determine the safest solution to the problem.

- Is there an exit nearby I can use to get everyone to safety? If people are flooding the exit, is there another avenue of escape? Identify as many as possible and mentally map out the best approach to each.
- Is there a place I can get everyone to that would provide appropriate cover or concealment? Identify as many as possible.
- If there is a break in the gunfire, is there something nearby I could use as an improvised weapon to subdue the shooter? If not, is there an opportunity to escape? How?

These visualization techniques are crucial when it comes to planning your best course of action. By imagining different scenarios as we move through our environments and envisioning various outcomes, we better prepare ourselves to act should the need arise. Remember that it's essential to think through each of these scenarios to the most desirable conclusion: to escape safely. Over time you will start to see the benefits of these drills and how these what-if games can significantly decrease your reaction time and improve your level of awareness.

7.5 Take Action

Every violent encounter consists of two separate battles: the one we fight in our minds before the confrontation and the actual physical conflict. The doubt and insecurity that accompany these encounters can create a losing mindset and cause you to give up long before things turn physical. People often give in or lose their focus because they let those negative feelings creep in and take over. Let's face it: bad things often happen to good people. It's important to understand that you may sometimes find yourself in horrible situations with little or no warning. If that happens, you have to push negativity aside and focus on the best way to react. At this stage, it's more often than not the case that your ability to act amid those feelings of doubt will be what saves your life.

You now have a good understanding of what choices you'll be faced with during a violent encounter and how situational awareness and visualization techniques can give you the time and space you need to avoid these encounters altogether. But let's imagine for a moment that you get caught up in something that was outside of your control. Imagine being on vacation in unfamiliar territory and suddenly finding yourself surrounded by an unruly mob. You saw the violence and mayhem start to unfold but soon realized that complete avoidance was impossible. How you compose yourself and react under these circumstances is critical to your survival.

Much of how you react to violence will be dependent on the amount of information you took in prior to the attack. Things like exits, cover, concealment, or improvised weapons that can be used to create distance are all critical features that need to be noted during your scans, but these aren't things that we usually consider when we're just out trying to have a good time. Now the question presents itself: how do we train ourselves to pay closer attention to these details without becoming hypervigilant or stressing ourselves out? The answer is simple—you just turn it into a game.

I use a simple counting drill to keep my awareness levels up while simultaneously taking note of useful features within the environment. Below is a list of tasks you can complete mentally any time you're out in public. You can do these exercises at home or while you're familiarizing yourself with a new environment. It takes discipline and conscious effort, but it becomes instinctive after a while and dramatically improves your chances of spotting a bad situation early.

- When you walk into a room, make it a habit to count all the exits and memorize their locations.
- Count the number of people in your general area, be it a restaurant, train, or parking lot.
- When counting, make sure to look at people's hands. The hands are what can hurt you.
- When walking down the street, periodically stop at a crosswalk or storefront and take a casual look behind you. Count the number of people who appear to be paying attention to what you do.
- Identify and count the number of items you could use as improvised weapons.
- When you're in a parking lot, count the number of cars with people sitting in them. How many of those cars are running?

Remember that it's not so much what you're counting but the act itself that gives you purpose and keeps you in tune with your environment. Think back to the way criminals choose their victims. In step four of the PROD, "Defenses," predators ask themselves, "Does this person display any visible signs of defenses? Do they look strong and capable? Are they alert to their surroundings and unlikely to allow an unwanted approach?" If they think you may be too much to handle in an altercation, they're more likely to shift their attention to someone else. These counting exercises provide you with options and the information you need to react appropriately, but they also require close observation and concentration. They keep your head up and give you focus, making you look more situationally aware and much less appealing to a potential attacker.

Key Points:

- Don't be a target.
- Predators can generally be broken down into two basic groups: resource predators and process predators.
- For a predator, target selection can be completed in as little as seven seconds. In that short span of time, a predator can accurately determine the following:

  ○ Their initial perception of how you will react during a violent encounter
  ○ The amount of risk you pose to them
  ○ The amount of observable value you possess
  ○ Your visible defenses

- These four factors, Perception, Risk, Observable Value, and Defenses, are what I refer to as the PROD.
- Basic movements that suggest signs of weakness are:

  ○ Short, shuffling strides when walking
  ○ Not swinging the arms in proportion with the stride
  ○ Exaggerated side-to-side movement when walking
  ○ Head facing at a downward angle when walking

- Basic movements that signal someone who's confident and capable are:

  ○ Medium to long stride when walking
  ○ Arms swinging in proportion to their stride
  ○ Body movement in vertical alignment, which was viewed as a strong and determined walking pattern
  ○ Head level and eyes visible when walking

- Situational awareness will require that you have a good understanding of your environment, how people dress and act, the general mood in a particular location, and a basic knowledge of the local customs.
- Once you've become accustomed to your surroundings, it's time to start looking for actions that fall outside of what is considered normal behavior. These actions are referred to as baseline anomalies and may include the following:

  o Hidden hands
  o Inexplicable presence
  o Target glancing
  o A sudden change of movement
  o Inappropriate clothing
  o Seeking a position of advantage
  o Impeding your movement
  o Unsolicited attempts at conversation
  o Heavier than usual breathing
  o Appearing tense
  o Posturing
  o Pupil dilation
  o Excessive sweating

- There's science behind your body's natural reactions to fear, even if you haven't consciously registered the fact that you're afraid. This is commonly referred to as intuition.
- If faced with a violent encounter, you have four options:
  1. Avoidance
  2. Escape
  3. De-escalation
  4. Confrontation

8

Security Considerations

Now that you have a pretty good grasp of the mechanics of situational awareness, it's time to move on to how this information gets applied in various settings. Although the scenery may change, the one thing that remains consistent is the need for awareness and the ability to identify potential problems before they can become a threat to your safety.

Here's another story from my first book that I feel illustrates the importance of situational awareness while traveling. When I was a young soldier stationed in California, I took a weekend trip to San Francisco with a few of my friends. We had all just gotten back from a thirty-day field problem in Twenty-Nine Palms and desperately needed to shed our sand-filled uniforms and hit the big city to blow off some steam. Keep in mind that I'm from the very small town of Sylvatus, Virginia, and this was my first trip ever to a place that had buildings over five stories tall. Getting off that bus and walking around downtown San Francisco blew my mind and sent my level of distraction through the roof. One night, after a considerable amount of dancing and drinks, I split from the group and decided to walk back toward the hotel. I didn't know my way around the city, and since this was well before Google Maps, I got seriously turned around. It didn't take long to figure out that I was lost and needed a cab to get me back to the hotel, so I pulled my wallet from my pocket to count my remaining money. Before I knew it, I was lying flat on my back, and the guy who had hit me was running away with my cash. This guy had obviously been watching me for a while, just waiting for the right opportunity to strike. I gave chase for a couple of blocks but quickly realized I was being led further into a bad part of town, so I swallowed my pride and let it go. Fortunately, a wise old staff sergeant of mine had taught me to always keep extra money and my military ID in the bottom of my shoe for just such occasions. I was able to catch a cab and make it safely back to my room with nothing more than a bruised ego and a few crumpled dollar bills. Looking back, I had made several mistakes that night. I had been drinking and separated from the group. I was unfamiliar with my routes, showed visible signs of distraction, and openly displayed value. Now let's take a look at the situation from the attacker's perspective by using the PROD method we discussed earlier.

- Perception: I was a lost tourist.
- Risk: I had been drinking and was visibly distracted, posing little risk to a potential attacker.
- Observable Value: I publicly pulled my wallet from my pocket and began counting out money.
- Defenses: I was alone and distracted, displaying minimal defenses.

As you can see, based on what we've covered so far, I was the perfect soft target. The lessons I learned that night were hard-won, but things could have been much worse. Lucky for me, this guy was a resource predator who was just looking for some quick cash. Despite the ridiculous amount of teasing I took from my friends, I recovered quickly from my injured pride and made the conscious decision to never put myself in that situation again.

I tell that story to illustrate how a change in venue and attitude can make an enormous impact on your personal safety. For thirty days prior to that event, I had been Gary Quesenberry, the soldier: ever vigilant, alert to danger, and constantly on the lookout for attacks from outside. Then, just a few short days later, I was Gary Quesenberry, the hard-partying tourist without a care in the world. You can clearly see how that shift in attitude led me into trouble. That's the same mistake many people make as they prepare to head out on vacation. Their desire to shed the weight of their day-to-day lives can often affect their ability to make sound decisions. It's perfectly acceptable to want to leave those responsibilities behind for a little while, but the need for good judgment and situational awareness only increases once you step outside your front door. That means that there are also aspects of situational awareness that apply to your mode of travel. Let's take a look at those now.

8.1 On the Road

According to a recent AAA Travel survey, nearly 100 million Americans set out on family road trips during the spring and summer of 2019. This number is reflected all over the world as people begin to strike out in search of adventure and relaxation. Hopefully, at this point, everyone understands the importance of drivers' safety and emergency preparedness on the road, so we're going to steer clear of those topics and focus on the aspects of travel safety that are directly impacted by  predatory violence. Let's start by taking a look at some areas along the road where situational awareness plays a significant role in your safety:

1. **Rest stops:** Roadside rest areas can provide travelers with a much-needed break from long hours in the car and offer up an opportunity to use the restroom, stretch your legs or enjoy a picnic lunch, but rest areas can also be dangerous. Criminals often target rest-stop visitors out of sheer convenience. Rest stops are generally in remote locations away from police stations and offer easy access to interstate highways for quick getaways. It's natural for criminals to assume that vacationers in rest areas, especially those traveling with children, will be easily distracted and often have a car full of valuables such as cash, credit cards, and electronic devices. The severity of rest area crime runs from petty theft—such as purses being snatched from hooks in restroom stalls—to strong-armed robbery and muggings, all the way to carjacking and homicide.

Here are a few helpful tips to increase your defenses and keep you safe the next time you find yourself in need of a quick pitstop.

- Completely avoid highway rest stops after 11:00 pm.
- If you must stop at night, try to find rest stops with dedicated security. This is usually noted on the rest stop signs before the entrance.
- Only park your vehicle in well-lit areas.
- If you are traveling with someone, accompany each other to the restroom area.
- Always lock your vehicle and have your keys ready when you return to it.
- As you approach your vehicle, look around and under the car and glance into the back seat before getting in.
- Rest stops, especially after dark, are no place to catch up on text messages and returned phone calls. Keep your phone in your pocket and your head up when walking to and from your car.

2. **Gas stations:** Gas stations come in all shapes and sizes, from locally-owned small stations to large chains. I always recommend that travelers stick with the larger chain stations that offer well-lit pump stations, surveillance cameras, and indoor restrooms.

3. **Restaurants:** There's not much to worry about here, but I always recommend requesting seating near windows with unobstructed views of the parking lot and your car. Although crime inside the restaurant may be rare, quick smash-and grab-robberies aren't outside the realm of possibility, especially if you have a car full of valuables that are easily visible to passersby.

4. **Roadside attractions:** Who doesn't love a good roadside attraction? During the road trips I've taken with my family, we've made impromptu stops at gold mines, ghost towns, an old Jessie James hideout, and the world's largest concrete dinosaur. Some roadside attractions are small and don't attract much attention, but some are larger and appeal to a wide range of both travelers and criminals. It can be safely assumed that people pulling over to take in these sights will naturally have cash or credit cards for souvenir purchases, making them a likely target for pickpockets and thieves.

These are just a few of the places you may find yourself along the road where your level of awareness could serve as a deterrent to crime, but your lack of awareness could possibly make you a target. Aside from paying close attention to your surroundings and keeping a lookout for things that may seem out of the ordinary, here are a few other tips that can help to keep you and your family safe:

- Only stop in areas with sufficient lighting.
- Once you're safely parked, immediately check your cell phone and verify that you have coverage in that area. If you don't, keep driving.

- When you leave your car, make sure you have your cell phone with you, but leave your valuables locked safely in your vehicle. Remember, showing observable value increases the likelihood that criminals could target you.
- If you're traveling with others, always walk together. Moving in a group makes you much less appealing to predators. If you're traveling alone, try your best to avoid rest areas at night. Opt instead to take your breaks at well-lit gas stations where there's an attendant on duty or at a restaurant.
- Never sleep in your car. If you get tired while driving, try to find an affordable hotel or campground along your route. You may have to spend a little money, but the safety they provide is well worth the extra cost.
- Always research your route as part of your planning phase. This allows you to pick the safest options for your stops well in advance of your trip.

8.2 In the Air

As a federal air marshal, you could say that I've become somewhat familiar with air travel, but even after nineteen years on the job, some of the things I see people try to get away with onboard an aircraft still surprises me. Some people assume that just because everyone onboard their flight has passed through security screening that the danger of crime inside the aviation domain is minimal. Those people couldn't be more mistaken. In the aftermath of COVID, air travel has become more dangerous and unpredictable than ever. Add alcohol and anxiety medications to those already growing frustrations, and you have a recipe for some entertaining mid-air confrontations.

According to the Federal Aviation Administration, from January 1st through May 24th of 2021, there were roughly 2,500 reports of unruly behavior by passengers. Fully 1,099 of those led to investigations by law enforcement. That's up from only 146 investigations in 2019.[6]

Aside from the standard post-COVID inconveniences, there is still the potential for serious violent crime aboard commercial aircraft. From hijackings to drug smuggling and human trafficking, the aviation industry remains a viable means of carrying out violence against the broader public. My team and I have personally been involved in human trafficking cases where young women were forcefully transported overseas from the United States. Fortunately, we had the training and recourses we needed to spot these actions and stop them. But not everyone has the benefit of that training. The question you may þe asking is, "How do I, as a common traveler, best protect myself and my loved ones from the possibility of inflight violence?" As with most things, the answer to that lies in situational awareness.

The first thing you need to consider is the actual possibility of mid-flight crime or violence. Although the chances of another 9/11-style attack are not negligible, they're also slim. On the other hand, someone becoming aggressive or violent with a member of the flight crew is much more likely. In any event, your main goal during an in-flight encounter will be to protect yourself and those traveling with you. The best way to do that is to be paying attention when it happens, then knowing what actions are most appropriate based on the circumstances. Let's look at a few situations you could possibly encounter during a flight.

Inquisitive passengers: We'll start with something simple. If you've ever flown before, I'm sure you know the type: that meddlesome person next to you throwing out questions faster than you can answer. In most cases, you can just chalk that one up to nervous chatter and a fear of flying, but there are people who will use the convenience of a long flight stuck next to a perfect stranger to collect information. My

---

6. https://www.faa.gov/data_research/passengers_cargo/unruly_passengers#:~:text=The%20repercussions%20for%20passengers%20who,violation%20for%20unruly%20passenger%20cases.

wife once sat next to a "very nice man" on a short flight from Las Vegas to Sacramento. During that two-hour flight time, he collected enough of her personal information to track her down and call our house. As it turns out, his intentions weren't criminal. He just wanted to rope my wife into a "get rich working from home" scheme. That was simple enough to shut down, but not every conversation turns out to be so innocent. Be cordial but cautious when it comes to answering personal questions from strangers. One trick I used to avoid questioning from my fellow passengers was to put on my headphones as soon as I took my seat. I rarely had anything playing on them because I needed to hear what was happening around me, but the presence of those headphones kept me out of a lot of unwanted conversations.

Intoxicated passengers: As a federal air marshal working out of the Las Vegas Field Office, I sometimes felt that dealing with drunken passengers was the sole purpose of my job. Unruly travelers excited about their chances of hitting it big in Vegas could sometimes get out of control and cross the gap between tipsy tourists and violent offenders. When this happened, it was usually the innocent person stuck next to them that had to call for assistance. If you ever find yourself in this situation, your best bet is to just excuse yourself to the lavatory and bring the problem to the attention of a flight attendant. They're trained to handle those situations, and by removing yourself from the equation, you give yourself the distance you need to remain safe should things turn violent. If you're unable to slip past your intoxicated seatmate, just hit the flight attendant call button and draw some attention to the situation.

Petty theft: If you've ever been on an airplane, you've seen this play out. A person sits down and immediately starts unpacking and setting up their space. Laptop, iPhone, iPad, headphones, Kindle . . . people tend to wrap themselves in this digital cocoon to ensure they can pass the time without giving much thought to the reality of their situation. Being stuck in a tin can with a couple hundred strangers at thirty thousand feet can do that to a person, but the presence of observable value (remember the PROD) can also entice theft. Here are a few tips to help keep your valuable safe:

- Keep your electronics and other valuables packed away until their needed.
- Always carry a small personal bag that will fit under the seat in front of you. That way, all of your valuables can be stored somewhere you can keep an eye on them.
- If you have to get up to use the lavatory during the flight, take that bag with you or have a known traveling companion keep an eye on it for you.

- Never store valuables in the overhead bin, or allow other passengers to move your luggage once you've put it away.
- Once the flight lands, be sure to take inventory of all your belongings. (This is where those packing lists come in handy.) If something of value is missing, be sure to bring it to the attention of a flight attendant before the other passengers exit the flight. They're usually happy to help. If you realize something is missing once you've exited the plane, it's almost impossible to get back onboard, and the chances of recovering your item are severely diminished.

Physical assaults: Hopefully, you're never the target of a violent assault onboard an aircraft, but assaults do happen, and sometimes innocent passengers can find themselves stuck in the middle of it. Your ability to protect yourself and those traveling with you will be dependent on where you're seated and how quickly you get away from the situation. When booking your flight, always try to reserve an aisle seat. You may enjoy sitting next to the windows and admiring the views, but in the event a fight breaks out next to you, you're trapped. If aisle seats are unavailable, try to get an exit row. Aside from the added leg room, this also gives you more space to escape a violent situation should one erupt during the flight.

Sexual assaults: As horrible as this may sound, sexual assaults do occur on commercial flights—particularly among young female passengers traveling alone. If someone sitting next to you becomes overly friendly or tries to put their hands on you, immediately remove yourself from the situation. It doesn't matter if the seat belt sign is on or if the flight is experiencing turbulence; get yourself away from your aggressor by any means necessary and bring the situation to the flight crew's attention. Cause a scene if you have to, but never let yourself fall victim to someone else's depravity.

Another thing to consider here is traveling with children. Often mix-ups during the booking process can lead to families being separated. NEVER allow younger children to sit alone without the

supervision of at least one parent. In most cases, the flight attendants will go out of their way to keep families together, but in the unusual event that's impossible, I recommend removing your family from the flight and rebooking. The inconvenience of the delay is much better than the possible alternative.

Hijackings: The Federal Air Marshal Service started small back in 1961 with only a handful of sworn agents. Back in those days, hijackings were pretty common. Between 1968 and 1972, there were 130 hijackings on American air carriers alone. The hijackers were typically driven by personal gain or just looking for safe passage to places they weren't supposed to go. They would demand that a flight take them to a place like Cuba, then demand hundreds of thousands of dollars in ransom money before they would release the passengers. For years, airlines mostly gave in to these demands because they felt customers would find enhanced security at the airport more of an inconvenience than the possibility of a hijacking. Things changed significantly after four commercial aircraft were taken over by al-Qaeda terrorists and used as steerable weapons of mass destruction on September 11th, 2001. Now air marshals number in the thousands and serve on both domestic and international flights to detect, deter, and defeat acts of terrorism.

In truth, federal air marshals can't possibly cover every flight into and out of the United States. Given that unfortunate fact, what actions should you take if you ever find yourself in a violent situation where the lives of everyone onboard and countless lives on the ground may be in jeopardy? To answer that question, let's look at how passengers reacted to an attempted bombing in late 2001 onboard American Airlines flight 63.

On that routine flight from Paris to Miami, British terrorist Richard Reid attempted to detonate explosives he had concealed in his shoe. There were no air marshals aboard that day, but luckily, Reid's "shoe bomb" failed to detonate. Sweat had soaked through his socks and into the device, making it almost impossible to ignite. Once Reid realized things weren't going as planned, his attempts to set off the improvised explosive became more erratic and drew the attention of an alert flight attendant.

Eric Debry, forty-two, a French tour operator traveling with his wife and two children, was taking a nap when he heard a commotion in the row in front of him.

"I need help here! I need help here!" the flight attendant shouted as she struggled with Reid.

Debry said he instinctively jumped out of his seat and grabbed Reid's shoulders to control him.

"Two other guys jumped on him and took his legs . . . We grabbed his arms; we grabbed his legs. We tied him up with everything we had . . . with our belts."

Noticing that the improvised explosives were concealed in Reid's black high-tops, passengers and crew tore off the shoes and placed them in a safe area towards the back of the plane. From that point, doctors traveling on the flight injected Reid with sedatives they had found in the onboard medical kit. Reid was subsequently arrested, fined two million dollars, and sentenced to three consecutive life sentences in prison.

No one boarded flight 63 with the intention of fighting and subduing a terrorist hellbent on destroying the plane, but that's what happened. Awareness, teamwork, communication, and determination all came together that day to accomplish a difficult task with no prior warning or coordination. In the event you ever find yourself in a situation like the passengers of flight 63, the important thing to remember is that you as an individual may not have the skills to stop a terrorist attack, but the flight will be full of people willing and able to help. Flight attendants are trained to respond to these types of events, so if you see something suspicious, bring it to their attention. On top of that, there will more than likely be doctors, nurses, off-duty police officers, or military personnel onboard. Communication will be instrumental in making sure everything gets handled effectively, so don't be afraid to speak up. If there are federal air marshals onboard, trust me, they'll take charge quickly and let you know precisely what you should be doing. Listen to what they tell you.

Key Points:
- Situational awareness also applies to your mode of travel.
- When you're on the road, increase your level of awareness at rest stops:

- o If you must stop at night, try to find rest stops with dedicated security.
- o Only park your vehicle in well-lit areas.
- o If you are traveling with someone, accompany each other to the restroom area.
- o Always lock your vehicle and have your keys ready when you return to it.
- o As you approach your vehicle, look around and under the car and glance into the back seat before getting in.
- o Rest stops, especially after dark, are no place to catch up on text messages and return phone calls. Keep your phone in your pocket and your head up when walking to and from your car.
- Gas stations
  - o Stick with the larger chain stations that offer well-lit pump stations, surveillance cameras, and indoor restrooms.
- Restaurants
- Roadside attractions
  - o Only stop in well-lit areas.
  - o Once you're safely parked, immediately check your cell phone and verify that you have coverage in that area. If you don't, then keep driving.
  - o When you leave your car, make sure you have your cell phone with you, but leave your valuables locked safely in your vehicle.
  - o If you're traveling with others, always walk together. Moving in a group makes you much less appealing to predators.
- Never sleep in your car.
- Always research your route as part of your planning phase.
- Some security issues you may face during a commercial flight are:
  - o Inquisitive passengers
  - o Intoxicated passengers

- Petty theft
- Physical assaults
- Sexual assaults
- Hijackings

PHASE THREE——Arrival

"My destination is no longer a place, rather a new way of seeing."
—MARCEL PROUST

9

On-site Security

NOW THAT YOU'VE ARRIVED safely, it's time to start thinking about securing your position. Much like the preparations you made at home, once you arrive at your destination, it's essential to establish a secure base of operations so you can enjoy your vacation without spending too much time worrying over the technical aspects of your personal safety. This all starts as soon as you step foot into your lodgings. Once your base is set, you can begin building rings of security that extend beyond your immediate surroundings and into the public spaces you plan to spend time in. We'll eventually get much deeper into all of that, but for now, let's just stick with securing your new accommodations.

Your base of operations is where the rest of your on-site security plans will be set and implemented, so it needs to be a place you feel comfortable. From it you can allow yourself to relax from time to time and recharge for your next excursion. Air marshals spend countless hours in the confines of a hotel. Not every country we traveled to was friendly, so going out and exploring wasn't always an option, but the need for security was ever present. Over the years, the process of checking into and securing my personal space became second nature. This routine, once perfected, becomes an essential element of personal safety and, when paired with situational awareness, allows you to enjoy yourself without being overly worried about outside threats.

Before we get into the details of securing your hotel room, there are

a few things that you want to consider well before you ever accept your room key. They will serve to put you in the safest possible position once you start to settle into your new environment.

- Research your location. Carefully choose the area that your hotel will be in. Hotels near police stations—or, if traveling internationally, near the embassy building—are always preferable. You can also do a quick internet search to assess the crime rates in various parts of the cities you'll be staying in.
- Research your hotel. Try to stick to well-established hotels with good security and stay with major hotel chains such as Sheraton, Hilton, and Marriott. Most major hotel chains have existing relationships with local cab services, restaurant chains, and

emergency response personnel, which comes in handy whether you're looking for a popular local pub or help with a security concern.

- Ask for a room on the third, fourth, or fifth floors. Rooms on the first two floors are easily accessible to criminals, so always make sure that you're at least on the third floor. Staying beneath the sixth floor also allows you an option for a quick escape through windows while minimizing the risk of injury. Plus, it grants easy access to emergency personnel such as fire and EMS, which may need a ladder to extract you from your room.

- Have the desk clerk write your room number down for you without announcing it. You never know who may be eavesdropping when you're in the hotel lobby. Don't take unnecessary risks by allowing the desk clerk to announce your room number to anyone who may be listening.

- Corner rooms are preferable. They give you the best view of your surroundings and generally place you closer to the emergency exits and service elevators.

- If you're traveling with a large group, make sure to collect everyone's room numbers so you can contact them quickly in the event of an emergency.

Now that you're checked in, you should familiarize yourself with the ground floor layout before proceeding to your room. You'll want to identify the security office, fire exits, and any access points to underground parking structures. By memorizing the general layout of the ground floor, you'll minimize confusion and save time should you need to make a hasty retreat from the property.

Once you've made it to your assigned floor, you'll want to do the same thing. Familiarize yourself with the layout and note any emergency stairwells, phones, alarms, or fire suppression devices like extinguishers or hoses. These things go unnoticed by most hotel guests, but they're critical to your safety, so don't overlook them. Once you're comfortable with the layout, make your way to your room. It's now time to secure your belongings and set up your base of operations.

I've spent a big part of my adult life living out of hotel rooms. They're generally clean, comfortable, and reasonably secure. But there are specific things you'll want to check before you start unpacking your bags:

- Many hotels offer valet or porter services to assist with moving your luggage to your room. If that's the case, make sure to keep the door propped open while the hotel staff is inside your room. If you're traveling alone, it's a good idea to keep the porter available while you check the room over.
- If there is a safe in your room, ensure that it's operating correctly.
- Check that the windows and balcony doors close and latch properly.
- Ensure that all deadbolts and latches are appropriately installed and operational.
- Make sure that all light switches and bulbs are functioning the way they're supposed to.

If you found anything wrong during your inspection, make sure you bring it to the porter's attention or call the front desk to either have the issues addressed or be moved to a different room. Once you're satisfied with everything, you can see the porter to the door, give them their tip, relax, and unpack. This is when you should be getting accustomed to your new surroundings and settling in. There are also several things you'll want to keep in mind as you unpack.

- When you unpack, keep everything neat and organized. Knowing where and how everything is placed inside your room will make it easier to detect tampering.
- Never leave your room without securing your jewelry or electronics in the room's safe. Remember to use those fireproof bags you packed for the trip.
- All other belongings should be secured in your locked luggage.
- Always secure your valuables and double-check that the door latches behind you when leaving your room.
- Keep the "do not disturb" sign visible outside your door. This usually indicates that someone is inside the room resting, which can deter unwanted entry.
- Leave the television or radio on to give the impression that someone is still in the room.
- If you leave the room for any reason, use that Scotch tape you packed. Once outside the room, place a small piece of the clear tape along the bottom of your door near the floor. Stretch a piece of tape from the outside of the door to the door frame. It's practically unnoticeable, but if someone opens your door while you're away, you'll see that the tape has been disturbed and know that someone has been inside your room before you reenter.
- Staying somewhere new can be disorienting, especially at night, so always have a flashlight readily available.
- If someone knocks on your door, always check the door peep. If it's obscured, or you can't see who's on the other side, do not open the door. Call the front desk to ask if they've sent someone up to your room. If they haven't, and you weren't expecting anyone, request hotel security immediately.
- When you're inside the room alone or sleeping, use your rubber door wedges and motion alarms to add an extra layer of security.

Once you've completed those tasks, you're all set. Now it's time to set up and test your communications equipment before striking out to familiarize yourself with the surrounding area.

Key Points:

- Your base of operations is the place from which the rest of your on-site security plans will be set and implemented, so it needs to be a place where you feel comfortable.
- Always remember to:
  - Research your location.
  - Research your hotel.
  - Ask for a room on the third, fourth, or fifth floors.
  - Corner rooms are preferable.
  - Have the desk clerk write your room number down for you without announcing it.
  - If you're traveling with a large group, make sure to collect everyone's room numbers so you can contact them quickly in the event of an emergency.
- Memorizing the general layout of the ground floor, you'll minimize confusion and save time should you need to make a hasty retreat from the property.
- Familiarize yourself with the layout of your assigned floor and note any emergency stairwells, phones, alarms, or fire suppression devices like extinguishers or hoses.
- When you unpack, keep everything neat and organized.
- Never leave your room without securing your jewelry or electronics in the room's safe.
- Keep the "do not disturb" sign visible outside your door.
- Leave the television or radio on to give the impression that someone is still in the room.
- When you're inside the room alone or sleeping, use rubber door wedges to add an extra layer of security.

10

Communications

IN 2003, ARON RALSTON PACKED up his mountain bike and left home for the canyon lands of southeast Utah. There he planned to explore the depths of Bluejohn Canyon, a thirteen-mile day hike. Aron was an experienced climber and outdoorsman who had served as a member of the Albuquerque Mountain Rescue Council. He had tackled plenty of trails tougher than the one he was about to face, so he set out early with only his backpack, one liter of water, and two burritos. He knew there would be little to no cellphone signal in the canyon, so he didn't bring a phone, and since the hike was just a quick eight hours, he failed to let anyone know where he was going. Little did he know that an unforeseen accident was about to strand him at the bottom of the canyon for five days, and change the course of his life forever.

Aron was descending into a deep sandstone slot when he accidentally dislodged an 800-pound boulder. The boulder pivoted and pinned Aron's arm against the wall of the canyon. The next second, the pain struck. "If you've ever crushed your finger in a door accidentally," he says, this was "that times one hundred." In an "adrenalized rage," he "cursed like a pirate" for forty-five minutes before reaching for his water bottle. As he drank, he had to force himself to stop. "I realize this water is the only thing that's going to keep me alive," he says. Having failed to tell anyone where he was going, he knew he wouldn't be found. "I put the lid back on the water bottle and gathered myself. It was like, all right, brute force isn't going to do it. This is the stop-think-observe-plan phase of rational problem-solving. I have to think my way out of here."

After two days spent fruitlessly chipping away at the rock with his knife, Aron devised a clever but futile system of pulleys with his climbing equipment to hoist the boulder clear. After realizing that nothing was working to free the boulder, Aron came to a stark and sickening conclusion: he was going to have to remove his own arm.[7] I'll spare you the gory details, but five days after being trapped by the boulder, Aron emerged from the canyon, dehydrated, delirious, and missing the lower portion of his right arm. He had constructed a tourniquet with the hose from his water bladder and stumbled upon three Dutch tourists who gave him water and helped him out of the canyon. Soon afterward he was picked up by a search-and-rescue helicopter dispatched by his family to look for him. Ralston still enjoys the solitude of his outdoor adventures, but now when he goes out hiking or climbing, he almost never goes alone, and he certainly brings his cellphone. Whether you're planning a quick day hike like Aron, or an international vacation, communication should be a critical part of your planning. Not only does it allow you the peace of mind that comes with being able to stay in touch with your support system, it can possibly be the key to your safe return.

When it comes to domestic travel, spotty coverage areas or a lack of Wi-Fi may be your biggest communication concerns. If you're the adventurous type like Aron, you may often find yourself in places where your cell phone is completely useless. In those cases, it's crucial

---

7. Patrick Barkham, "The Extraordinary Story behind Danny Boyle's 127 Hours," *The Guardian*, Dec. 15th, 2010, https://www.theguardian.com/film/2010/dec/15/story-danny-boyles-127-hours.

that you provide your friends or family members with a little information before you go:

- Where you're headed and what route you're taking
- How long you'll be away
- When you plan to return

If you'll be setting up a base of operations in a hotel or campground, make sure there is a contact number you can give to your support team. That way they have a number to call in case there's an emergency at home and you can't be reached. In addition, long-range two-way radios are useful if you're staying relatively close to home, or if you're traveling with a group in areas where cellphone coverage is minimal.

If you plan on traveling internationally, things can get a little more complicated, and expensive. Before you ever step foot in an airport, it's imperative that every member of your group (depending on their age) have a working mobile device so they can stay in touch both in the air and once you've reached your destination. According to Verizon.com, here are a few things you need to do before you leave so your communications stay up and running.[8]

- **Use a temporary international plan:** Different mobile providers offer varying degrees of coverage in different countries, and it's important to determine whether your current plan and device will be compatible with the network wherever you're going. In some cases, it may be prudent to invest in a temporary international travel plan, as this may lead to lower charges overall.
- **Unlock your mobile device:** A locked mobile phone is one that has a software lock on it, preventing you from using it on another carrier's network. An unlocked device is simply one that lacks this restriction. If you'll be going to an area without adequate service

---

8. https://www.verizon.com/info/technology/international-cell-phone-use/.

from your carrier, you may need to temporarily switch carriers. With a locked phone, however, this is not possible.

• **Purchase a prepaid international phone:** Some service providers offer prepaid international plans with phones that are already unlocked and ready for use abroad. These come with several different plans, from those with unlimited long-distance calls to those with standard pay-per-minute option

• **Replace your SIM card:** A SIM (subscriber identity module) card is a tiny memory chip that stores data about your cell phone use. A SIM card also stores data on its country of origin and the mobile carrier you use. These can be easily transferred from one mobile device to another, which makes switching mobile devices for international travel a simple process. By moving your SIM card to a new device, you are able to make and receive calls and texts with that device, as well as access cellular data. If you move your SIM card to a new device, your phone number will move over to the device that you put it in. Your old device will lose much of its functionality until the SIM card is returned to it. Alternatively, you can get a local SIM card, which means you will also get a local phone number. Getting a card from a local- or country-specific provider may be necessary to use the device, depending on your destination.

- **Use Wi-Fi enabled messaging apps:** Whenever possible, you may want to rely on Wi-Fi connections rather than cellular data as this will result in fewer extra charges to your account. While relying primarily on Wi-Fi may seem restrictive, there are many communication alternatives you can use via a Wi-Fi connection. This includes applications like:

  ○ Facebook Messenger
  ○ Google Hangouts
  ○ Skype
  ○ Telegram
  ○ WeChat
  ○ WhatsApp

In addition to tools such as these, you can also maintain contact with loved ones via social media apps such as Facebook, Instagram, or Twitter. Further, some cell phone providers, have Wi-Fi calling options, as well as mobile hotspots to enable Wi-Fi access on the go.

- **Keep your phone charged:** Reliable access to the online information and tools you'll need overseas requires more than just a carrier plan; it also means keeping your phone charged and in good working condition. Even the best international data plan can be rendered useless if you don't have methods to actually keep your mobile devices charged. The first thing to consider is finding the right electrical plug adapter for your travel destination. There are fifteen different plug types, and different countries use varying combinations of these types. Invest in appropriate adapters so that you can reliably charge your mobile devices during your travels. You can find international wall charger kits for pretty cheap and they'll make your life a lot easier. Another point to consider is the possibility of bringing an external battery pack to keep your phone charged when you don't have access to an electrical outlet. Battery accessories come in a wide range of shapes and sizes, including portable power banks and even phone cases with built-in batteries. Keeping one of these on hand can be a lifesaver when you're far from home.

Now that your communications are all set up and you know you can reliably connect with both the members of your group as well as your support team back home, it's time to start learning a little more about what's around you. This process is known as area familiarization.

Key Points:

- Any time you'll be away in an area with unreliable cellphone coverage or limited Wi-Fi, it's crucial that you provide your friends or family members with a little information before you go.
  - Where you're headed and what route you're taking
  - How long you'll be away
  - When you plan to return
- If you'll be setting up a base of operations in a hotel or campground, make sure there is a contact number you can give to your support team. That way they have a number to call in case there's an emergency at home and you can't be reached.
- Long range two-way radios are useful if you're staying relatively close to home, or if you're traveling with a group in areas where cellphone coverage is minimal.
- If you plan on traveling internationally, there are a few things you need to do before you leave so your communications stay up and running.
  - Use a temporary international plan.
  - Unlock your mobile device.
  - Purchase a prepaid international phone.
  - Replace your SIM card.
  - Use Wi-Fi enabled messaging apps like:
    - Facebook Messenger
    - Google Hangouts
    - Skype
    - Telegram
    - WeChat
    - WhatsApp
- Keep your phone charged and in good working order.

11

Area Familiarization

Most of the work concerning area familiarization can be handled during your threat assessment. Using the State Department website, the CIA World Fact Book, and other sources of OSINT is a great way to learn about the regions you'll be visiting and collect any relevant information pertinent to your safety, but that's just the beginning. The real work starts as soon as your feet hit the ground at your destination. It's crucial that you be familiar with the area you're visiting. After checking in to your hotel and setting your base of operations, area familiarization is the next important step in establishing proper on-site security. You've already taken note of the basic layout of the lobby, your assigned floor, and your room. Now it's time to expand your reconnaissance to the area just outside your hotel. Here are a few tips to help you out:

1. Once you're back in the lobby, it's also a good idea to locate the concierge service desk as well as ATMs, public phones, and the business office. Concierge services are very helpful because they can assist in familiarizing you with the local area. They usually have city maps on hand and can provide you with reliable transportation to and from the hotel if needed.

2. If you're outside the country, be sure to find the distance and direction of the US embassy. You'll need proof of your citizenship to get in, so make sure you always carry copies of your passport and other identification. It's also a good idea to digitize these documents and place them on a secure flash drive that you can keep with you at all times.

3. Learn the locations of local hospitals, pharmacies, firehouses, and police stations.

4. Ask the concierge about any local areas that should be avoided or areas where tourists may not be welcome.

Once that's all completed, it's time to get out and start your grand adventure, but there are still a few things that you need to be aware of so you can move freely in your new environment without drawing unnecessary attention to yourself or your group.

Key Points:

- After checking in to your hotel and setting your base of operations, area familiarization is the next important step in establishing proper on-site security.
- If you're outside the country, be sure to find the distance and direction of the US embassy. You'll need proof of your citizenship to get in, so make sure you always carry copies of your passport and other identification. It's also a good idea to digitize these documents and place them on a secure flash drive that you can keep with you at all times.
- Learn the locations of local hospitals, pharmacies, firehouses, and police stations.
- Ask the concierge about any local areas that should be avoided or areas where tourists may not be welcome.

12

Cultural Awareness

BACK IN THE EARLY MONTHS of 1991, several of the guys from my unit and I were selected to serve with the 24th Infantry Division during Operation Desert Shield/Desert Storm. They needed a few artillery-men to augment one of their units, and I was lucky enough to be chosen. Much to my surprise, there was quite a bit more to deploying overseas than just hopping on a bird and flying to Saudi Arabia. A considerable amount of training had to be completed before we were considered "battle-ready." First, we were injected with more shots than I care to remember and flown from Fort Ord, California, to Fort Knox, Kentucky. There we were issued new weapons and desert uniforms, given extensive training in nuclear, biological, and chemical warfare and refresher courses in patrolling and basic first-aid—all things we were familiar with. A small portion of our training consisted of something new to us, however. It was called cultural awareness training. Although there was a bit of eye-rolling when we were first told about it, the information we were provided about the part of the world we'd be operating in proved to be instrumental in working and communicating effectively with our Middle Eastern counterparts.

Cultural awareness also plays a vital role in personal safety when it comes to foreign travel. As Americans, we're sometimes blind to the fact that not everyone in the world follows the same rules, holds the same values, or enjoys the freedoms that we do here in the United States. When we consider traveling to a foreign country, we tend to project our cultural norms onto other populations, which can lead to confusion, miscommunication, and in the worst cases, violence. For example, when we first landed in Saudi Arabia, the shock was immediate. The temperature had been cool, and it was raining when we left Kentucky, but when we landed at King Fahd International Airport just outside Dammam, it was well over one hundred degrees. It didn't take long for us to realize how important it would be for us to stay hydrated, so we found a food truck, run by a couple of locals, that had tubs full of ice-cold water. The guy in front of me grabbed a water bottle and handed it to the man behind the counter, who quickly became irate. He was yelling angrily and waving his arms. We were all very confused by what had happened, but someone who had been there a few days longer than we had pointed out the mistake. The guy in line had inadvertently offended the man behind the counter by taking the water with his left hand. That's a big no-no in some Middle Eastern cultures because the left hand is considered unclean and should never be used to eat, drink, or hand things to other people. That was just one of many cultural lessons we were introduced to during our first week in-country. Not everyone reacted the same way to our lack of etiquette, but it was apparent that our cultural awareness training back in Kentucky had only scratched the surface of how different we really were.

Before you set off to a foreign location, I advise taking a few steps first to understand what's appropriate and what's not in the places you'll be visiting:

1. **Research your location:** To be most efficient, you should incorporate the cultural awareness portion of your research into your threat assessment. Then, during the intelligence briefing, pass that information along to anyone you may be traveling with.
2. **Watch the locals:** Keeping an eye on how the locals do things can save you a lot of embarrassment. For example, if you see people bowing instead of shaking hands, chances are bowing is the preferred form of greeting. This "watch and learn" approach to cultural familiarization also serves another purpose. By keeping your head up and taking note of the local customs, you're also developing a sense of the normal baseline behaviors in that area. This, in turn, makes you more alert and less likely to be approached by someone with predatory intentions.
3. **Pay attention to how people react to you and adapt accordingly:** I remember my first trip to Rome, Italy. We were being met by some local law enforcement officials inside the airport. As the team leader, I was approached by one of the officers, who happened to be a young female. I stuck my hand out for the standard American greeting but was shocked when she took my hand, leaned in, and kissed me on the cheek. I was taken aback and probably even blushed a little. This wasn't how professional law enforcement officers greeted each other in the United States, but she smiled, patted my shoulder, and said, "Welcome to Rome. You'll get used to it." She was right. By the time I retired, I was used to it, and that form of greeting became as natural to me as shaking hands. I became comfortable with cultural differences, and it made me a better air marshal.

I was only nineteen the day we landed in Saudi Arabia, but I was still traveling the world as a federal air marshal when I turned fifty. Over the years, I developed a pretty good understanding of cultural differences and how they affected the way I did my job, but what I came to realize was that one of the greatest joys in traveling is the process of learning. We're all so very different, and although we may not consider it, it's critical to our safety that we learn as much about the places and people we'll be visiting as we possibly can. As I mentioned earlier, how we carry ourselves and interact with people plays a significant role in the way we are perceived. If you decide not to immerse yourself in the local customs of the place you're visiting, you'll naturally stand out, and that can sometimes be a bad thing.

Key Points:

- Cultural awareness plays a vital role in personal safety when it comes to foreign travel.
- Before you set off to a foreign location you should understand what's appropriate and what's not in the places you'll be visiting. Here's what I recommend:
  - Research your location.
  - Watch the locals.
  - Pay attention to how people react to you and adapt accordingly.

13

Blending In

BLENDING INTO YOUR ENVIRONMENT and not sticking out like a sore thumb is a lot harder than it sounds, especially when you're traveling through foreign countries. In most cases, people naturally try to set themselves apart and stand out in a crowd. Our need to be noticed pushes us forward and helps us do things like land a job, make friends, and find a mate. Given that we're all so unique and different, how do we go about toning ourselves down so that we aren't so easily noticed?

Federal air marshals have perfected the art of blending in and going relatively unnoticed as they pass through the world's busiest cities and airports. A lot of the lessons we learned about blending in, we learned the hard way. During our initial training, there wasn't a lot of guidance on how to dress or act so we didn't draw attention to ourselves. Most of what we learned back then was through trial and error. One important lesson I learned was that 98 percent of the people you come into contact with are so absorbed in their own issues that they seldom have the time or inclination to pay any attention to you, so going unnoticed is easy when it comes to the general public. The thing you need to be most concerned about is not drawing the attention of the other 2 percent: the predators who have made a science of sizing you up and determining whether or not you should be their next victim.

Back in chapter seven, I mentioned how sociologists Betty Grayson and Morris Stein conducted a study in 1981 that cast new light on how criminals chose their victims. Grayson and Stein believed that potential victims were possibly signaling their vulnerability to attackers through their gestures, posture, and movements. The researchers set up video cameras on a busy intersection in New York City and recorded people walking by between 10 am and noon for three consecutive days. The tape was later shown to inmates who were incarcerated for violent offenses such as armed robbery, rape, and murder. The inmates were instructed to rate the people in the videos on a scale of one to ten, one being an easy target and ten being someone they would altogether avoid. The pedestrians that rated between a one and three were designated as easy or "soft" targets. The pedestrians rated between seven and ten were selected as hard targets and should not be approached. It's no secret that criminals prefer soft targets, but what I find most interesting about the study is that the criminals entirely ignored those pedestrians rated between four and six. When asked to relate what they remembered about the group in the middle of the scale, the inmates couldn't remember a thing about them. When it comes to blending in and not drawing attention to yourself, that middle range is where you want to be. In the federal air marshal service, this is known as being the "gray man."

There are a lot of misconceptions about what it means to blend in with your surroundings. Blending in is not hiding. It doesn't involve sitting in the dark corners of a room with your face hidden behind a newspaper. Blending in requires you to be familiar with your surroundings and use what you know about your environment to mimic the look and mannerisms of the people surrounding you. There are three primary aspects of blending in that you need to be familiar with if you're trying to vanish into the background.

1. **Clothing:** You always want to pick your clothing based on the environment, activity, and customs of the people around you. Another thing to consider when choosing appropriate clothing is your destination. When traveling to an unfamiliar city or country, you need to do your research and find out how the locals dress. One option is to pack light and buy your clothing from a local shop at your destination. I'm not talking about the t-shirt that says, "I went to Rome, and all I got was this lousy t-shirt." I'm talking about authentic native clothing that helps you look like you belong there. This brings me to my next point: identifying yourself as a tourist or, even worse, an American tourist, can cause a lot of unwanted problems when you're in a foreign country. In Europe, Americans are sometimes viewed as uncultured and obnoxious, so go out of your way to adopt the tone and mannerisms of the locals in the area you're visiting. Remember your cultural familiarization. You should also limit observable value by not wearing unnecessary items such as flashy watches, expensive purses, or camera cases when you're traveling. These items always identify you as a person who may have money and can make you a pretty appealing target. Your best clothing options are always comfortable, durable, and inconspicuous when blending in. Keep it simple, with no flashy colors or logos, and keep the color scheme muted and neutral.

2. **Body language:** When it comes to body language, confidence is king. Always look like you know what you're doing and where you're going, even if you don't. At the same time, you don't want to appear overly confident to the point of seeming aggressive. This can make you stand out in the crowd just as quickly as being excessively timid. Move deliberately and with a purpose. When you're in a group of people, naturally there may be some interaction, so if someone approaches you, be friendly but cautious. Don't avoid eye contact or go out of your way to dodge the conversation. If you'd rather be left alone and limit your interaction

with others, there are many ways to do that. When I was working on the plane, I would avoid conversation as much as possible with other passengers. As I mentioned earlier, my favorite technique for this is to just pop in a set of headphones and act like I couldn't hear anyone. You don't have to be listening to music or even have them plugged in, but the act of appearing busy helps to limit the amount of interface you have with others.

3. **Positioning:** By positioning, I'm referring to where you sit, stand, or move within your environment. For instance, someone who looks for a quiet, open corner in a cafe will naturally stand out more than someone who chooses to sit in the middle of the crowd. The same goes for movement. If you're positioned on the outskirts, you'll be noticed more quickly than if you moved within the crowd. When you isolate yourself, you become more vulnerable. If you don't believe me, just watch the Discovery Channel. Predators always hunt around the edges of a herd. I work and frequently move through airports and foreign countries. When traveling, I always try to strike a balance between being on the edges and being smack in the middle of a crowd. Suicide bombers typically try to make their way to the center of a crowd before detonating. This allows for maximum casualties and causes the most confusion. By positioning yourself between the outskirts of a room or group and the dead center, you're giving yourself a buffer from those direct-center attacks while maintaining your anonymity and proximity to possible escape routes.

There are plenty of ways to keep from standing out or marking yourself as a soft target. The things I've listed above help, but the most important thing you can do to blend in with your surroundings is just to be yourself. Be polite to those around you and smile when it's warranted. You can't move through life constantly looking like a stone-faced killer; it's unnatural, and it's no way to blend in. Don't try to adopt some ridiculous disguise or alternative personality. Trying too hard is counterproductive and makes you look even more out of place. By just being yourself, you act more natural and confident, which makes you much less appealing to predators. More importantly, looking like a natural part of your environment also gives you a better vantage point from which to observe your surroundings. That's the end goal here: to casually observe your environment and move from point A to point B, confident that you won't be caught off-guard or targeted by someone else due to your inability to blend in.

Key Points:
- Blending in requires you to be familiar with your surroundings and use what you know about your environment to mimic the look and mannerisms of the people surrounding you. There are three primary aspects of blending in you need to be familiar with if you're trying to vanish into the background:
  1. Clothing: Limit observable value by not wearing unnecessary items such as flashy watches, expensive purses, or camera cases when you're traveling. Your best clothing options are always comfortable, durable, and inconspicuous when blending in. Keep it simple, with no flashy colors or logos, and keep the color scheme muted and neutral.
  2. Body language: Always look like you know what you're doing and where you're going, even if you don't.
  3. Positioning: When you isolate yourself, you become more vulnerable. By positioning yourself between the outskirts of a room or group and the dead center, you're giving yourself a buffer from direct attacks while maintaining your anonymity and proximity to possible escape routes.

14

Spotting Danger

NOW THAT YOU'VE ESTABLISHED your base of operations and familiarized yourself with your new surroundings, it's time to have a little fun. You've worked hard preparing for this moment, and I know you're excited to get out there, but first, there are a couple of things you need to understand about situational awareness, tourism, and predatory violence.

According the ASU Center for Problem-Oriented Policing, tourism is an interactive relationship among tourists, local businesses, host governments, and communities. It is the United States's second-largest service industry (after health care) and directly or indirectly supports 204 million jobs. Still, it has also led to increased opportunities for and incidences of crime.[9] Like it or not, there has always been a relationship that exists between tourism and increases in crime. This relationship exists for several reasons. First, tourists are lucrative targets since they typically carry large sums of money and other valuables. Second, tourists are vulnerable because they are more likely to be

9. Ronald W. Glensor and Kenneth J. Peak, "Crimes Against Tourists," ASU Center for Problem-Orienting Policing, 2004, https://popcenter.asu.edu/content/crimes-against-tourists-0#endref1.

relaxed, off guard, or careless while on vacation. Crimes against tourists generally involve one of two scenarios:

1. The tourist is an accidental victim, in the wrong place at the wrong time, targeted as an easy mark.
2. The location is conducive to crime due to its nightlife, hedonistic culture, and the number of potential victims.

Although theft is the most common crime against tourists, they are also vulnerable to other crimes, including kidnapping, physical and sexual assault, credit card fraud, and street scams. As tourists' numbers grow, so too can local hostility toward them, thereby increasing the chances they will be cheated, robbed, or assaulted. Now, you may be asking, "How can all of this be avoided while still relaxing and enjoying yourself on vacation?" The answer lies in the understanding of situational awareness and how the different levels of awareness affect both your safety and your ability to lower your guard and relax.

No one can possibly walk around all day in a state of hypervigilance and still expect to unwind and have any fun. Hypervigilance and relaxation just aren't compatible. The trick is to understand the baseline behaviors of your new environment and apply the appropriate level of awareness based on the information you're receiving. Here's how it's done.

Situational awareness can be separated into five levels. These levels of awareness are most commonly referred to as "Cooper's Colors." The Cooper color code system of awareness was developed by Marine Corps Lieutenant Colonel Jeff Cooper and includes five conditions, or colors, that represent a person's mental state as they go about their daily activities. These five levels explain the general ranges of situational awareness and the psychological conditions associated with each level.

1. **Condition white:** In this condition, a person is entirely relaxed and unaware of what's going on around them. For instance, someone walking along staring at their cell phone while listening

to music through their headphones could be considered in condition white. They've effectively cut themselves off by blocking out all visual and auditory indicators they may receive from their surroundings. In the majority of cases, condition white is reserved for when you are asleep or when you find yourself in an environment that you assume to be completely free of threats, like your own home. Criminals generally target people they deem to be in condition white because their lack of awareness makes them look like easy prey. Suppose you are ever attacked while in condition white; the chances of escape are severely diminished because your attacker will have caught you off guard. Your actions at that point will be completely reactionary.

2. **Condition yellow:** This is a state of relaxed awareness and the condition that allows you to most effectively take in your surroundings and monitor baseline behaviors. You appear to those around you to be entirely comfortable in your environment while paying close attention to the sights and sounds that surround you. This condition of awareness does not constitute a state of paranoia or hyper-vigilance. Instead, you've simply upped your awareness to a level that would prevent you from being caught off guard.

3. **Condition orange:** At this stage, you have identified something that could be perceived as a threat, and you've narrowed your attention to that specific person or area. You quickly notice abnormal behaviors in others and shift your level of awareness to accommodate those actions. This is also the stage where you begin to put together spontaneous plans, and the anticipation of action starts to elevate your heart rate. Once the perceived threat has passed, it's easy to relax and transition from condition orange back to yellow.

4. **Condition red:** This is where you find yourself right before you act on your plans. In condition orange, you spotted a perceived threat and began the planning stages for an appropriate reaction.

In condition red, the threat has materialized, and it's time to put those plans into action. This is where the heart rate becomes more elevated, and the fight, flight, or freeze responses are triggered. Your body prepares itself for confrontation, and the adrenaline starts pumping into your system. Condition red is where your level of training has a significant impact on how the situation is resolved.

5. **Condition black:** Condition black is much like condition white in that you do not want to find yourself there when the fight starts. Condition black is characterized by an excessively elevated heart rate (above 175 beats per minute) and a complete loss of cognitive ability. A person in condition black lacks the power to process the information being taken in effectively and becomes utterly useless in terms of response.

When it comes to maintaining proper situational awareness, you always want to stay in condition yellow. You want to be in that casual yet observant state that allows you to take in as much information as possible without completely stressing yourself out. That's the only way you can effectively monitor your baselines while still allowing yourself to relax.

In chapter seven, we covered the basics of situational awareness and how to get "switched on." Now that you understand baseline behaviors and the different levels of awareness, you have a pretty good idea of how this all ties into your personal safety while on vacation. Now let's take a closer look at some of the crimes against tourists that people tend to fear most.

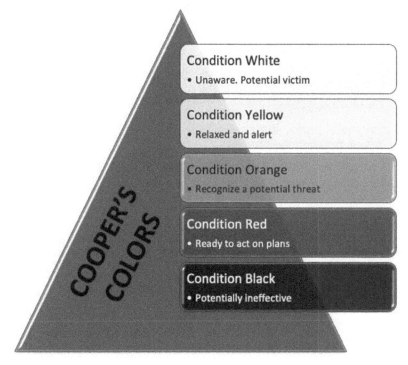

14.1 Acts of Terror

Terrorism is the unlawful use of violence and intimidation, especially against civilians, in the pursuit of political aims. Terrorism is a very real threat to world travelers, and over the past decade, terrorists killed an average of 21,000 people each year worldwide. Still, statistics show that the number of tourists killed annually by acts of terrorism is minimal. Here are a few facts to help ease your mind before your travels:

- The global death toll from terrorism over the past decade ranged from 8,000 in 2010 to as high as 44,000 in 2014. There has been a steady decline since then.
- In 2017, terrorism was responsible for only 0.05 percent of global deaths.

- Terrorism tends to be geographically specific. Ninety-five percent of terrorist-related deaths in 2017 occurred in the Middle East, Africa, and South Asia.
- In most countries, terrorism accounts for about 0.01 percent of deaths, but in countries that are considered conflict areas, this can be much higher.
- Globally, public concern about terrorism is high. In many European countries, about half of people surveyed said they are concerned about becoming a victim of terrorism.
- Media coverage regarding acts of terror can be disproportionate to its frequency and number of deaths.[10]

Part of staying safe while traveling will require you to understand where and when terrorist attacks are most likely to occur. Then it's just a matter of increasing your level of awareness when you find yourself in those situations. Remember, situational awareness is what will give you the time and distance you need to escape should things go wrong in your area. Let's take a look at some of the specifics:

Where:

- **Crowded places,** including train stations, sports arenas, markets, and shopping centers
- **Tourist attractions,** especially those frequented by foreign tourists
- **Places of worship,** such as mosques, churches, synagogues, temples, and shrines
- **Airlines,** for both hijacking and bombing
- **Government facilities,** including office buildings and military facilities
- **Identifiably Western interests, such as** embassies, consulates, airlines, foreign oil and gas infrastructure, premises of multinational

---

10. Hannah Ritchie, Joe Hasell, Edouard Mathieu, Cameron Appel, and Max Roser, "Terrorism," *Our World in Data*, July 2013 (Rev. October 2022), https://ourworldindata.org/terrorism.

companies (including employee residential compounds), and international schools

- **Places where Westerners gather;** these can include hotels, restaurants, nightclubs, and other entertainment venues catering to foreign clientele

When:

- **National holidays,** such as New Year's Day and Independence Day
- **Religious dates or observances,** such as Christmas, Easter, and Hannukah
- **Significant dates and anniversaries,** such as 9/11
- **During elections,** especially at political events such as rallies

I understand that travelers are often worried about terrorism in general, but don't let your perception of the world around you skew the reality. Travelers are much more likely to be victimized by criminals than they are to be caught up in an act of terror. The good news is that with proper situational awareness, both of these possibilities can be avoided if you're staying alert to your surroundings, watching out for baseline anomalies, and planning for avoidance or evasive actions.

14.2 Kidnapping

Even in the post-pandemic world of travel, there is an ongoing threat of kidnapping for ransom, especially in foreign countries. Although it's difficult to nail down specific statistics regarding abductions, hostageus.org estimates that roughly 300 Americans are kidnapped overseas each year.[11] To better protect yourself from being targeted, you must familiarize yourself with the various forms of kidnapping and where these crimes are most likely to occur.

---

11. *Hostage US*, "Information about Kidnapping," https://hostageus.org/media/information-about-kidnapping/.

Types of kidnappings:

- **Basic kidnapping:** This "traditional form of kidnapping involves the abductor leveraging the hostage to extract payment from a family member, employer, or country of origin in exchange for the hostage's release. Kidnapping for ransom is a significant source of income for both criminal and terrorist organizations, as they rely on this income to further their operations.

- **Express kidnapping:** This type of kidnapping is common in Africa and South America. This is a relatively short-term ordeal and generally only involves the kidnapper and the victim. The criminal will take the victim to an ATM and threaten them with violence if they don't withdraw the maximum allowable amount of money. The kidnapping will generally end when the victim can no longer withdraw any cash. Express kidnappings are designed to be quick and profitable for criminals and are almost always a crime of opportunity.

- **Virtual kidnapping:** This form of kidnapping is unique because it does not involve an actual abduction. The criminal will target a "victim" and gather as much personal information about that person as possible, usually through social media. They will then contact that person's family or employer claiming to have kidnapped them and demand a ransom for their release. The amount demanded is usually smaller to ensure quick payment. In most cases, the person who has been targeted is unaware that their loved ones are being manipulated back home.

- **Political kidnapping and ideological kidnapping:** This is usually considered the most dangerous form of abduction due to the wide range of motives and groups involved. The kidnappers often target their victims because of their political or ideological impact. This type of kidnapping usually corresponds with demands for prisoner swaps, withdrawal of forces, or propaganda targeting a particular religion or population.

Areas of Concern:

In April of 2019, Kimberly Sue Endicott traveled from her home in California to Uganda for a vacation. Kimberly had always wanted to visit Africa so she could witness gorillas living in their natural habitat. To her, this was a bucket-list trip, and she couldn't be more excited. That excitement soon turned to terror as she and her safari guide were kidnapped and held for $500,000 ransom.[12] That horrific encounter lasted for five days before Kimberly and her guide were released unharmed.

This incident prompted the State Department to implement a system in which travelers could be warned about the threat of kidnapping in various locations. As I mentioned in chapter two when we discussed threat assessments, the State Department already issues travel advisories for every country worldwide, with advice on crime, terrorism, civil unrest, natural disasters, health, and other potential dangers. In the wake of Kimberly's kidnapping, the State Department announced that it was also adding an indicator to show which countries have the highest risk of abduction. Now, any country with a risk of kidnapping will have the letter "K" on its travel advisory. According to the State Department, the goal is "to communicate more clearly to US citizens the risks of kidnapping and hostage-taking by criminal and terrorist actors around the world."

Before traveling abroad, I highly recommend referring to the State Department's website, travel.state.gov, for updates and threat warnings. Below is an excerpt from their site regarding travel to Uganda.

Uganda

Violent crime, such as armed robbery, home invasion, and sexual assault, is common, especially in larger cities including Kampala and Entebbe. Local police lack the resources to respond effectively to serious crime. The kidnapping of foreign citizens

---

12. Laura Begley Bloom, "35 Countries Where Americans Are Most Likely To Get Kidnapped," Forbes, April 25th, 2019, https://www.forbes.com/sites/laurabegleybloom/2019/04/25/35-countries-where-americans-are-most-likely-to-get-kidnapped/?sh=3f42574abdf1.

remains a concern, though such incidents occur infrequently. In April 2019, a US citizen was kidnapped in Queen Elizabeth National Park, in the southwest region of Uganda, near the border with the Democratic Republic of the Congo (DRC). The US citizen was later released unharmed. Additionally, there is a threat of terrorist attacks in Uganda and throughout the region. US citizens should avoid large public gatherings

As you can see, aside from the general rundown of crime in that area, the site even refers to Kimberly's kidnapping specifically. You must stay informed about the crimes being committed in the area you plan on visiting before you travel. Although this information is collected and discussed during your threat assessment and intel briefing, it's a good idea to refer often to the State Department's site for last-minute updates and emergency travel notices.

14.3 Street Crime, Scams, and Tourist Traps

One evening while relaxing in my room at the King George Hotel in Athens, I received a call on the room phone. This wasn't unusual. Most hotels give their arriving guests a courtesy call to ensure that their room is satisfactory, so I answered. The person on the other end of the line informed me that there was an issue with the credit card I had used to check-in.

"So sorry to disturb you, sir. The card you used at the front desk doesn't appear to be valid. The number was probably just entered into the system incorrectly. If you'd like, we can verify the number over the phone and straighten this out."

That request may seem reasonable at first, but there were several indicators that something was off. First, I never made the reservation. That was all taken care of through headquarters well in advance of the trip. Secondly, when I checked in, the lady behind the desk wouldn't have given me the room key had the credit card not been processed correctly. This all seemed a bit suspicious, so I offered to come down to the front desk to straighten everything out.

"No, no, no, we wouldn't want to disturb you any further. You can just give us the number over the phone, and we'll get this sorted out for you."

"I'll be right down," I said as the line went dead.

I then proceeded downstairs to investigate. Sure enough, the lady I had checked in with knew nothing about the problem with my credit card and informed me that there had been issues in the past with scammers watching as people checked in, then calling their rooms to try to get their credit card information. (This is why we never let the desk clerk announce our room numbers.) If they had gotten it, you could guarantee they'd have drained every cent they could from my account.

This type of scam isn't uncommon, even when traveling domestically. No matter where you go in the world, there will always be people looking to take advantage of others, but there are things you can do to protect yourself. Aside from exercising good situational awareness, you also need to familiarize yourself with some of the more common street scams that criminals try to run on unsuspecting tourists. Once you understand how these cons work, they become much easier to spot. Aside from the credit card scam I described earlier, here are ten of the more common scams you could encounter and how to avoid them.

1. **The unlicensed driver:** You tend to see this one just about everywhere, whether you're traveling domestically or internationally. Well-dressed and friendly drivers will meet you right outside the airport's secure area and offer to take you anywhere you'd like to go. This seems enticingly convenient as it helps you avoid long lines at the taxi stand and gets you where you need to go quickly, but beware. These drivers are unlicensed and unregulated. In most cases, they will get you where you need to go, but you'll pay nearly double the standard taxi fare.

   How to avoid it: Never accept the offers for a ride from someone inside the airport. If you plan on taking a cab, be sure to proceed to the authorized cab pickup location and wait in line there. There will usually be an attendant handy to show you to your cab.

2. **Broken taxi meters:** This scam is also pretty common, even among licensed cabbies. The driver will help you load your bags and then tell you that the taxi's meter is broken. They will then quote you a price for your destination. This may seem reasonable, but it will always be well above the actual rate. The cabbie can then pay the company and still pocket a few extra bucks.

   How to avoid it: Before you get into the cab, make sure of three things first.

   1. Is the cab's meter working correctly?
   2. Does the driver accept both cash or card?
   3. Does the driver have proper change on hand?

   Once you're in the cab, pull up the route on your phone or consult a local area map to ensure the driver is utilizing the quickest path to your destination.

3. **Your hotel is closed:** This one usually occurs once you're all loaded up and inside the cab. The driver will ask you where you're headed. If you give them the name of the hotel you're staying in, he will tell you a story about how the hotel is overbooked due to a big event or closed because of some unforeseen incident. Not to worry, the driver will offer up a suggestion on a much nicer hotel that has plenty of room. These hotels are usually local and way more expensive, and the driver will receive a nice kickback for bringing in new customers.

   How to avoid it: Call your hotel in advance and make sure they're open for business. Ask if they offer shuttle service and then schedule a pickup from the airport. If there is no shuttle and your taxi driver still insists that the hotel is unavailable, demand that he take you there anyway. He may seem offended, but that's okay. Pull up the route to your hotel on your phone because he's probably taking you the long way to make a little extra cash.

4. **Flowers for the lady:** This has happened to me in just about every country I've traveled in. Someone will approach you with offers

for flowers or some handmade trinket. They're very friendly, but if you decline their "gift," they will become persistent. Once you accept the gift, they will demand money or cause a scene to draw attention to you. In some cases, they will be working with a local shopkeeper who will intervene and demand that you pay the nice person for their hospitality. They usually escalate the pressure until the victim of the scam caves and hands them some money.

How to avoid it: Don't allow anyone to put anything on your body, and be extremely wary of accepting anything for free, especially in very touristy areas. Ignore them and keep walking.

5. **Let me take your picture:** You've more than likely found yourself in this situation, sightseeing in some touristy location with plenty of beautiful photo opportunities. Sometimes it's a struggle to get a good photo alone or even with a group without leaving someone out. That's when a helpful local will step in and offer to take a picture for you. Be very wary of these offers. In some cases, the friendly stranger will wait until they're in possession of your phone or expensive camera and run away with your goods.

   How to avoid it: This one can be tricky, so you'll have to read the situation. I've happily handed my phone over to other people for a group photo. But it's almost always me asking them for the favor, not them offering out of the blue. Busy city attractions are the riskiest places for this. If you have to, ask fellow tourists instead and then offer to return the favor.

6. **You dropped your ring:** This one has been tried on me just about every time I've visited Paris, but it happens all over the world. Here's how it works: you're walking around, checking out the sights when someone walks up beside you, bends over, and picks up a "lost" ring. They'll proclaim how lucky they are to have found such a beautiful ring but quickly tell you they have no use for it. After examining the ring and pointing out the "24kt" engraved on the band, they'll offer to sell it to you for a

reasonable price, but rest assured, the ring is a fake. They probably have twenty more just like it in their pocket.

How to avoid it: Never accept anything from strangers. If someone approaches you with something that obviously isn't yours, simply say you aren't interested and keep walking. They'll be persistent, so you have to be too.

7. **Fake ticketing:** Every vacationer has their list of "must-see" places. Unfortunately, many of these places are plagued by long lines and offer little opportunity for shade or water. Often, while you're searching for the end of the ticket line, a very official-looking tour guide will offer you a chance to purchase "express" tickets. These will allow you to skip the line but cost significantly more than your average ticket. If you choose to buy the ticket to avoid waiting in line, the guide will then point you in the direction of the "express entrance," which is usually far removed from where you're standing. In most cases, you'll arrive there only to find that there is no entrance or that your new ticket is a fake. The fake ticketing scam can be run on everything from bus tickets to tourist attractions and theatre seats, so be careful who you purchase from.

How to avoid it: Wait in the line and never buy tickets to anything from someone off the street. Some attractions do offer express tickets to avoid the long wait, but those are usually purchased in advance through their official website.

8. **Money exchange:** This one is easier to pull when you're overseas and unfamiliar with the local currency. A shopkeeper or taxi driver will give you less change than you are supposed to get, or they will quickly exchange the fifty euros, say, you gave them for a five and claim that you gave them the wrong bill. They'll then demand more money in exchange for not calling the police.

How to avoid it: Familiarize yourself and your fellow travelers with the local currency before the trip. If there is still any question about what denomination you're handing over, just take your time. Double-check the amount, and don't allow yourself to be rushed or pressured.

9. **The bump and grab:** Probably one of the oldest scams in the book. This one usually happens in crowded areas or on trains and buses. Someone will bump into you and make a scene to draw your attention to them. This usually involves escalating levels of either apology or verbal abuse. Once your attention is drawn elsewhere, their accomplice will take the opportunity to pick your pockets or rummage through your purse or luggage. **How to avoid it:** Accidents happen, and chances are you will be bumped and jostled around in some of the more crowded areas. Be cautious when someone makes a big show of the incident. Don't let your attention be drawn away from your belongings. Be sure to keep purses and backpacks in front of you when in crowds, and don't allow easy access to your belongings by the people behind you.

10. **Fake police officers:** In just about every one of the scams I've mentioned so far, there is the potential for law enforcement involvement. If you feel like you're being taken advantage of and the matter escalates, the offended local will inevitably call for the police. Once they arrive, there will be a lot of pressure put on you to pay up or be taken into custody. If the police officers seem uninterested in your side of the story, that's usually because they're not real cops and are working with the locals to take your money. They'll usually ask to see your passport. If you hand it over, they'll refuse to give it back until you pay.

    How to avoid it: Never hand over your wallet or passport. Request that the officers show you their identification and have your phone handy so you can call the local police to confirm their identity. Or tell them your passport is locked up in the hotel safe, and they'll need to accompany you to your hotel. This isn't an unreasonable request. If they don't allow it, simply walk away.

This list only represents some of the more common scams you could encounter during your travels. These are tried and true cons that have been around forever, but criminals are constantly finding new and inventive ways to prey on tourists. Always keep your eyes open and your situational awareness level high when you're in large crowds or near densely populated tourist attractions.

14.4 Civil Unrest

One frightening reality for travelers in major cities is the likelihood of civil unrest. According to the Armed Conflict Location and Event Data Project (ACLED), between May and August of 2020, there were more than 10,600 demonstration events across the United States. Over 10,100 of these involved peaceful protesters. Fewer than 570, or approximately 5 percent, involved demonstrators engaging in

violence.[13] Civil unrest can occur anywhere, and although your chances of encountering violence during a protest are low, your need to remain vigilant remains high. During your threat assessment, it's always good to familiarize yourself with an area's political situation before you leave home. Try to find out if there have been any recent violent demonstrations at your chosen destination, then research what the protests were about and how the authorities handled those situations.

Suppose you ever inadvertently get caught up in a demonstration. In that case, your priority is to get out of there as quickly and safely as possible. You don't want to attract any undue attention or become an attractive target, especially if things turn violent. Here are a few helpful tips that can keep you and your family safe should you ever find yourself in the middle of such a situation.

13. ACLED, "Demonstrations and Political Violence in America: New Data for Summer 2020," September 3, 2020, https://acleddata.com/2020/09/03/demonstrations-political-violence-in-america-new-data-for-summer-2020/.

- If you find yourself caught up in a protest or riot, keep to the edge of the crowd where it's safest. A good way to avoid being identified as one of the demonstrators is to keep well away from the people actively participating.
- At the first opportunity, break away and seek refuge in a nearby building or find a suitable doorway or alley and stay there until the crowd passes.
- When leaving the fringe of the demonstration, just walk away—don't run or draw attention to yourself.
- If you are caught up in the crowd, stay clear of glass shop fronts, stay on your feet, and move with the flow.
- If pushed to the ground, try to get against a wall, roll yourself into a tight ball, and cover your head with your hands until the crowd passes.
- Remember to keep calm—the crowd should sweep past in a short space of time.
- If there is gunfire, drop to the ground, cover your head and neck, and lie as flat as possible.
- If you are arrested by the police/military, do not resist. Go peacefully and contact your embassy to help resolve your problem.

If escape is impossible and you do get caught up in the chaos, there's a chance that you could be confronted or threatened. Your initial inclination might be to engage in an either physical or verbal confrontation. However, the safest choice is almost always to de-escalate the situation. Try to stay calm, respond clearly, obey police commands, and make every attempt to leave peacefully. If you're inside your accommodations when a demonstration breaks out, adhere to the following protocols:

- Do not leave your lodgings or go into the street.
- Contact your embassy or consulate and advise them of the situation and your whereabouts.

- If you are in a room with doors or windows opening onto the ground floor, ensure that all windows and external doors are closed and locked.
- If you hear gunfire or explosions outside, stay away from the windows. Do not be tempted to watch the activity from what you consider a safe distance. Draw the curtains or blinds to prevent shards of broken glass from entering your room.
- Move to an inside room, which will provide greater protection from gunfire, rocks, or grenades.
- Stay in contact with hotel management to receive updates on the situation outside.

If you're in a car and run into a crowd of protesters, the following actions are often your best bet for remaining safe:

- Never drive through the crowd.
- If you find yourself in the path of a crowd, turn down the nearest side road or turn around and drive away immediately.
- If you cannot drive away, park the car, lock it, and leave it where it sits. Move immediately to shelter in a side street or open building away from the crowd.
- If you don't have time for this, stop and turn the engine off. Lock the doors and remain calm. Be sure not to show hostility or anger. Get on the phone with local authorities immediately and notify them of your situation.

Being caught up in an unexpected demonstration can be frightening, especially in areas that you're unfamiliar with. Remember that situational awareness and preparedness are what will give you the time and distance you need to identify and react to these types of incidents effectively, but even then, there will always be the potential for things to go wrong. That's why it's crucial to preplan your responses to as many unforeseen circumstances as possible. This process is known as contingency planning.

Key Points:

- Crimes against tourists generally involve one of two scenarios:
  1. The tourist is an accidental victim, in the wrong place at the wrong time, targeted as an easy mark.
  2. The location is conducive to crime due to its nightlife, hedonistic culture, and the number of potential victims.
- Situational awareness can be separated into five levels. These levels of awareness are most commonly referred to as "Cooper's Colors" and explain the general ranges of situational awareness and the psychological conditions associated with each level.
  - Condition white: In this condition, you are entirely relaxed and unaware of what's going on around you. Your actions at that point will be completely reactionary.
  - Condition yellow: This is a state of relaxed awareness and the condition that allows you to most effectively take in your surroundings and monitor baseline behaviors.
  - Condition orange: At this stage, you have identified something that could be perceived as a threat, and you've narrowed your attention to that specific person or area.
  - Condition red: This is where you find yourself right before you act on your plans. In condition red, the threat has materialized, and it's time to put those plans into action.
  - Condition black: Condition black is characterized by an excessively elevated heart rate (above 175 beats per minute) and a complete loss of cognitive ability.
- If you're ever caught in a protest or riot keep to the edge of the crowd where it's safest.
- If you're inside your accommodations when a demonstration breaks out, do not leave your lodgings or go into the street.
- If you're in a car and run into a crowd of protesters, never drive through the crowd. Turn down the nearest side road or turn around and drive away immediately.

15

Contingency Planning

CONTINGENCY PLANNING is nothing more than anticipating the possible problems you may encounter during your vacation and devising plans to minimize the impact of those problems. Some problems are simple: Is the ticket line at the tilt-a-whirl too long? Let's go have an early lunch and check back in an hour when things have died down. Other problems may be more complex. You're in a crowded area and become separated from your family. What plan do you have in place to reunite safely? The range of issues you may encounter while traveling is endless, so don't drive yourself crazy with this. Remain flexible on the most minor problems and focus your attention on the contingencies that could directly affect the safety and security of the people you're traveling with. Issues like medical emergencies, separation, and unforeseen problems at home are the ones that could have a devastating impact on your travel plans, so we're going to focus on those for now. The long line at the tilt-a-whirl will work itself out.

Making a contingency plan consists of five steps:

1. Identify the security risks at each stage of your travel. Remember to keep your focus on those things that impact safety.

2. Prioritize risks based on severity and likelihood. The chances of becoming separated in a crowd are much more likely than the chances of a terror attack, so start planning for the most likely incidents first.

3. Develop plans that allow you to address those risks while minimizing their impact on your trip. Keep your plans simple.

4. Brief the other members of your party on all emergency plans. If you're traveling with young children, be sure to keep them informed, but not to the point of making them afraid.

5. In the event of an emergency, monitor the effectiveness of your plan and create new ones as the need arises. As the old saying goes, plans are nothing more than a point from which to deviate when things go wrong. Be flexible in your planning, and keep in mind that even the best-laid plans will need to change if you find them ineffective.

This process can apply to just about any situation, but for the purpose of this book, we're going to take a look at four different emergencies that would require some contingency planning and walk through a few solutions for each. We'll start with the most common: the medical emergency.

15.1 Medical Emergencies

From minor scrapes and bruises to broken bones and stab wounds, medical emergencies are a significant concern for anyone traveling through unfamiliar territory. The key to effectively addressing these issues is preparation. In most cases, you can minimize the impact of unforeseen medical problems by preparing for them in advance of your trip. Before you leave home, you should always:

- During the planning phase of your trip, be sure to identify local hospitals and drug stores near where you'll be staying.
- Contact your health insurance provider to see what type of coverage you have in the area you'll be staying. If your coverage is

minimal, or you're traveling to a less developed region, you may consider purchasing travel health and medical evacuation insurance.

- Research any mandatory or recommended vaccinations that may be required and make sure you're up to date on all of your shots.
- Pack a basic first-aid kit. Be sure to include items such as Imodium for upset stomachs and anti-nausea medications for travel sickness.
- Make sure you pack enough prescription medications to cover your entire trip, plus a few extra days to be on the safe side.
- Once you arrive at your destination, be sure to double-check the locations of hospitals and drug stores.
- Find a local grocery store to stock up on fresh water and sunscreen.

These steps will keep you prepared for minor medical issues while you're away, but don't neglect your research. Make sure everyone in your party knows where the local hospital is and how to contact emergency services should the need arise.

15.2 Separation

This is probably one of the most common events families face while away on vacation. Especially if you're traveling with smaller children. Talk to any adult, and they will tell you a story about how they were once separated from a parent and how that separation caused both anxiety and fear. Crowded areas like amusement parks, festivals, concerts, and beaches are all rife with distractions. Your attention can be drawn away quickly, and within seconds members of your party can find themselves completely lost. It's vital that you've trained everyone in what they should do before something like this ever happens. Here are a few things you should cover with them before you begin your trip:

- Establish an agreed-upon meeting point before leaving your hotel room. If you become separated from your group, get there quickly and don't let anyone distract you.
- If no meeting point was established, freeze—moving around too much could cause you to become more lost.
- Let younger children know that they shouldn't be afraid to yell your name. You'll be shouting their name too until you're reunited.
- Start looking for the "good guys." If it's taking too long to find your group, start looking for someone like a park employee or security officer who can help.

These four simple steps can make a stressful situation much less difficult to handle. Still, you must let your younger children know that if you get separated from them, you will be working diligently to reconnect. Fear and panic can cause kids to act erratically, worsening the problem. Separation from the group isn't as frightening with older children. They usually have cell phones and naturally want to strike off on their own. Parents can establish preset meeting times and places to have their child "check in" or set mandatory call times so that you know they're okay. If for some reason they feel that they're in danger, have them contact you or emergency services immediately.

15.3 Incidents at Home

To fully enjoy a trip away, you need to be able to forget about what's happening back home for a while. That's what your support team is for, right? Of course it is, but planning for unforeseen contingencies back at home should be a part of your trip planning process. Here are a few things you should do before you leave to ensure you stay well informed about what's happening while you're gone.

- Make sure each member of your support team has the contact information of every group member. That way, if one phone is down, they have backup numbers should someone needs to be contacted.
- When you book your travel tickets, be sure to pay for the travel insurance that comes with them. That way, if your plans have to change or your vacation gets cut short, you can avoid the hassle and fees that come with trying to change a nonrefundable ticket.
- Before you leave, make sure you have basic home maintenance numbers programmed into your phone: plumbers, electricians, general handyman services. If a pipe breaks back home or the water heater goes on the fritz, you want to be able to get the repairs completed right away.

Knowing what's happening back home helps to put your mind at ease and allows you to relax. It also frees up a little of the mental bandwidth you need to keep tabs on what's happening around you. Remember, distractions can cause you to lose focus on what's important right now, like your personal safety. If you're out and about and something happens back home that needs your immediate attention, move to an area where you feel secure (preferably your base of operations) and handle the situation as best you can.

15.4 Getting Stranded

On Christmas Eve, 2021, thousands of airline passengers were stranded in airports around the world due to a spike in COVID cases, staff shortages, and severe weather. According to the flight tracking website flightware.com, a total of 2,118 flights were canceled worldwide, including 500 flights originating from or headed to the United States. Over 5,700 flights were delayed.[14] As a federal air marshal, I've been stranded overseas more often than I care to remember. Delays and cancelations when heading home can happen with little or no warning. Things like inclement weather, civil unrest, terror threats, and volcanic eruptions have all impacted travelers and wrecked any chance they had of getting back home on time. Although some delays in your return may be more severe than others, it's crucial you have a plan for extending your stay a little longer than expected and a support system that will have your back and keep everything running smoothly back at home until you return. If your travel plans include any mode of transportation that could incur a delay or cancelation, there are a few things you can do ahead of your trip to help minimize the impact of a late return.

- Whenever possible, choose nonstop travel. If avoiding connections in airports or train stations isn't feasible, try to aim for longer layover times to compensate for potential delays.
- Trips during busy travel periods like winter holidays or spring break increase your chances of experiencing delays. When traveling for a holiday event, consider arriving early and leaving late.
- You can't control the weather, but you can pay attention to it and exercise some level of common sense. If you're traveling by air, don't book a connecting flight destined for the Midwest in

---

14. https://flightaware.com/.

the middle of winter, and avoid the Gulf of Mexico during hurricane season. Keep in mind that weather-related cancellations are more common for flights from smaller towns, while larger international airports will have departure priority.

- Pack for the occasion. Be sure you have extra clothing or access to laundry services while you're away. Nothing is worse than being stranded in an airport for two days with no clean clothing.
- If you or a member of your group take regular medications, be sure to pack extra in case of delays or cancelations.
- Be sure to bring light packable blankets to use in the event you get stranded inside an airport, train station, or bus terminal.

Although it's impossible to account for every conceivable contingency, it's important that you think through the possibilities and prepare yourself for the unforeseen. Remember that failing to plan is planning to fail. You never want to put yourself or those you're traveling with in a situation where your safety could be jeopardized due to a lack of preparation.

Key Points:

- Contingency planning is nothing more than anticipating the possible problems you may encounter during your vacation and devising plans to minimize the impact of that problem.
- Making a contingency plan consists of five steps:
    1. Identify the security risks at each stage of your travel. Remember to keep your focus on those things that impact safety.
    2. Prioritize risks based on severity and likelihood. The chances of becoming separated in a crowd are much more likely than the chances of a terror attack, so start planning for the most likely incidents first.
    3. Develop plans that allow you to address those risks while minimizing their impact on your trip. Keep your plans simple.
    4. Brief the other members of your party on all emergency plans. If you're traveling with young children, be sure to keep them informed, but not to the point of making them afraid.
    5. In the event of an emergency, monitor the effectiveness of your plan and create new ones as the need arises. As the old saying goes, plans are nothing more than a point from which to deviate when things go wrong. Be flexible in your planning, and keep in mind that even the best-laid plans will need to change if you find them ineffective.

16

Maintaining Control

THIS MAY SEEM a bit off-topic, but it's every bit as important to your personal safety as any of the situational awareness topics we've covered this far. Murder, terrorism, kidnapping, and robberies all top our list of concerns when traveling through unfamiliar territory, but the fact of the matter is this: you're much more likely to be injured or killed on vacation through a lack of personal control than you are by any of those other things. Every year people are injured or worse on their vacations because they decide to take unnecessary risks with drugs, alcohol, and even taking selfies. (That last one isn't a joke, as you'll see later on.) Simply minimizing your intake of intoxicants and thinking through your decisions can go a long way in keeping yourself safe. Now let's take a look at some of the things likely to get you seriously hurt on vacation. The following list is comprised of four of the most common causes of death among vacationers.

1. **Traffic accidents:** The easiest way to reduce your chances of dying on holiday is surprisingly straightforward: wear a seat belt. The most common cause of death for travelers anywhere in the world is a traffic accident. This can include anything from crossing the

street to moped and bike rentals. If you're going to take it upon yourself to manage your own transportation through unfamiliar territory, be certain that you thoroughly understand local laws and traffic patterns.

2. **Drugs and alcohol:** People tend to indulge themselves a little more than normal when they're on vacation. Younger travelers in particular are drawn to destinations that promote a "party scene," where access to drugs and alcohol are more convenient. According to the US National Institute on Alcohol Abuse and Alcoholism (NIAAA) approximately 1,825 college students between the ages of eighteen and twenty-four die each academic year from accidental alcohol related injuries. During spring break, 44 percent of college girls and 75 percent of college guys get drunk on a daily basis. Approximately half of college students binge drink—many will drink to the point of passing out at least once during their vacation. Unfamiliar surroundings and drug use are a recipe for disaster when it comes to personal safety, so always exercise some level of moderation. If you plan on drinking in excess, have someone with you who can keep an eye on things and get you back to you room safely once the night comes to a close.

3. **Drowning:** The CDC and US State Department cite drowning as the third most common cause of death for Americans abroad. Stay safe by swimming with a buddy and never go into the water alone and, again, lay off the booze. As for scuba diving, don't do it—unless you're an experienced diver or have a qualified, reliable instructor. No matter how tempting it may seem, avoid jumping or diving into unfamiliar waters. You never know what's below the surface. Shallow water can hide rocks and reefs that can cause head and spinal cord injuries that can easily lead to drowning. If you plan on swimming during your vacation, be sure to exercise some caution and don't put yourself into a situation where rescue would be impossible. Be sure to use the buddy

system whenever possible and only swim in authorized locations.

4. **Selfies:** As the world emerges from COVID-19-related isolation, selfie-related fatalities have skyrocketed. In 2021, there were twenty-four reported deaths associated with daredevils looking for the perfect selfie, compared to just seven in 2020. Falls are the most common cause of selfie fatalities, responsible for a third of all deaths. Since researchers began tracking selfie-related deaths in 2011, India has recorded the most with 184. The US came in second with twenty-five and Russia placed third with nineteen.[15] The solution to this one is simple: never risk your life for a cool picture. There will be plenty of opportunities for some amazing memories while you're away without jeopardizing your safety. I'm sure your social media followers will understand if you fail to capture that image of you hanging over the edge of the Grand Canyon.

15. Dan Avery, "Number of People Killed While Taking Selfies TRIPLES After Lockdown Lifts, with Most Dying By Falling or Drowning During Attempt to Get the Perfect Snap of Themselves," Daily Mail, October 4th, 2021, https://www.dailymail.co.uk/sciencetech/article-10057683/Number-people-killed-taking-selfies-triples-lockdowns-lift.html.

Vacations are meant to be fun and relaxing, and there's nothing wrong with indulging in the local party scene. Just be sure to exercise the proper amount of caution and moderation when you do. Everyone will want to hear about your adventures when you return home, but no one wants to hear you tell about them from a hospital bed.

Key Points:
- Every year people are injured or worse on their vacations because they decide to take unnecessary risks on vacation.
- Simply minimizing your intake of intoxicants and thinking through your decisions can go a long way in keeping yourself safe.
- Four of the most common causes of death among vacationers include:
  1. Traffic accidents
  2. Drugs and alcohol
  3. Drowning
  4. Selfies
- Be sure to exercise the proper amount of caution and moderation when you're away on vacation.

17

Heading Home

SO HERE WE ARE, at the end of what was hopefully a safe, relaxing, and enjoyable trip. It's hard to come to grips with the fact that your vacation is over, and very soon you'll have to settle back into the routine of day-to-day life back at home. At this point, your mind starts looking ahead to the tasks that need to be completed once you return, the backlog of unanswered emails, yard work, missed meetings, and encroaching deadlines. As your adventure draws to a close, it's easy to get sidetracked by the mental to-do list you're creating in your head, but now's not the time to lose focus. You're still far away from home and possibly have a long journey ahead of you. For that reason, the need for safety and security is just as important now as it was when you left home.

Back in 2001, Progressive Insurance conducted the first survey to research where most traffic accidents happen. Findings revealed that 52 percent of accidents happened within five minutes of the motorist's homes and 77 percent happened within fifteen miles. Although this study was conducted over two decades ago, newer research continues to support the original claim. This study raises the question: why do so many accidents occur close to home as opposed to far away? The answer is simple. Familiarity. Motorists can become so familiar with their commute that they "zone out" or go into "auto-pilot" while driving, which can cause all kinds of problems and lead to some pretty serious consequences. This same thing can happen to vacationers returning home from a trip. Once the bags are packed and you start looking forward to sleeping in your own bed, it's easy to become focus locked on that end goal and neglect the things that are most important in the moment, like security. Here are a few things I do to avoid focus lock and maintain my situational awareness on the way home.

1. Call your point of contact back home before you leave to ensure that everything on that end is running smoothly. That'll help to put your mind at ease and allow you to put more focus on the return trip.

2. Conduct one last equipment check before you leave your lodgings. Finding out that you left your laptop in the hotel after you've made it to the airport will only cause problems and draw your attention away from your surroundings.

3. Allow yourself plenty of time to get to where you need to be. Rushing unnecessarily increases the chances of leaving things behind and adds to the stress of traveling.

4. If you're traveling with a group, call one last meeting to ensure everyone is prepped and ready to go. Reemphasize the need to remain vigilant on the return trip and remind everyone of the need to be situationally aware.

These four simple steps can go a long way in alleviating some of those last-minute distractions and help to keep you focused on getting home safely.

Key Points:

- To avoid focus lock and maintain situational awareness on the way home:
    1. Call your point of contact back home before you leave to ensure that everything on that end is running smoothly.
    2. Conduct one last equipment check before you leave your lodgings.
    3. Allow yourself plenty of time to get to where you need to be.
    4. If you're traveling with a group, call one last meeting to ensure that everyone is prepped and ready to go.

18

Post-travel Considerations

COMING BACK HOME from a vacation can be like jumping headlong into ice-cold water. It's a shock to your system, but there are things you can do to mitigate that shock and ease back into your old routine with minimal disruption to the relaxed state of mind you worked so hard to achieve. But remember, that relaxed state of mind can also impact your situational awareness. If your physical body is back at work but your mind is still on vacation you can lose focus on your surroundings and put yourself at risk. Here are seven things you can do to help smooth your transition and avoid the stress of becoming distracted or overwhelmed.

1. **Check in with your support team prior to heading home:** As I mentioned in the last chapter, checking in with your support team gives them time to prepare for your return and allows them to fill you in on anything of importance that may have happened while you were away. Knowing ahead of time what you'll be walking into back home (be it good or bad) will minimize any concerns you may have prior to your departure and allow you to focus on your safe return.

2. **Tidy up your backlog:** Once you're back home, chances are you'll be greeted by piles of unopened mail and other items left behind by your support team. Rather than ignore these things, take a few minutes to process them. Open envelopes, chuck junk mail, file what's important, and get reorganized. The longer you wait, the more likely these things will still be sitting on your dinner table later in the week.

3. **Sort through your voice mail and email:** Before you start playing catch up, update your away messages on your voice mail and email accounts if you set that up in advance. This is a task that's easily overlooked, so it's a good idea to attend to these items as soon as you can. Now is also a good time to check and write down your voice messages and clear out your mailbox.

4. **Review your schedule:** You've been away for some time, so you'll probably need a little reminder as to what is going on with work or school. Scan your calendar for the next couple of days to get an idea of upcoming meetings, due dates, projects, and other concerns. You'll be better prepared for the days ahead and won't be completely caught off guard when it comes to getting ready for that big meeting on Monday morning.

5. **Prioritize what comes next:** As you review your emails, postal mail, voice messages, and the like, you'll be reminded of all the stuff you were working on before you left home. Instead of working on the first item that crosses your path, make a conscious effort to prioritize your work.

6. **Pace yourself:** You may feel the urge to work on three different things at the same time in order to catch up, but this is not the most efficient approach. You'll only confuse and stress yourself out. Make a point to focus on one task at a time. You've just come back from a nice relaxing vacation; why stress yourself out if you can avoid it?

7. **Cut yourself a break:** Returning to work after a vacation is a transition period. Don't beat yourself up over how long it's taking you to catch up on things. It may take several days for you to finally get readjust, and that's perfectly fine. Stay calm, focused, and relaxed. You'll be back to your old routine before you know it.

Eventually, you'll slip right back into your old routine, but those lingering effects of time spent away with family and friends will help to fuel you through the monotony of day-to-day life. Take a moment each day to reflect on the places you saw and the things you experienced. Scroll through a few pictures on your phone. Remind yourself that there's a great big world out there and you're a part of it. A big international vacation may not be within your reach, but I'm sure there are plenty of hidden treasures close to home that you can explore on your next long weekend. Take advantage of each opportunity you have to get away and reconnect with the people and places that are important to you.

Key Points:

- There are seven things you can do to help smooth your reentry and avoid the stress of becoming overwhelmed once you return home.

  1. Check in with your support team prior to heading home.
  2. Tidy up your backlog.
  3. Sort through your voice mail and email.
  4. Review your schedule.
  5. Prioritize what comes next.
  6. Pace yourself.
  7. Cut yourself a break.

Conclusion

"And the purpose of life, after all, is to live it, to taste experience to the utmost, to reach out eagerly and without fear for newer and richer experience."

—ELEANOR ROOSEVELT

FOR NEARLY TWO DECADES, I traveled the world in service to my country. I've been very fortunate to have seen the places I've seen and experience the richness of diversity our world has to offer. I often get asked, "What are the most striking differences you've noticed between Americans and people from other countries?" The answer to that question may not be what you'd expect. I had been in Saudi Arabia, Iraq, and Kuwait before I ever turned twenty-one. I experienced some very stark cultural differences there, but I also witnessed acts of kindness, generosity, and courage that aligned with the same personal values I held. Once I began my travels as a federal air marshal, I found that it wasn't our differences that were so striking, but our similarities. No matter where I find myself in the world, there are things I can identify with and relate to. Most people are good and want to be treated that way. People are curious, kind, and helpful; they work hard and care deeply for those they love. They're patriotic, fierce, and capable of unimaginable heroism when the need arises. But our similarities don't stop at those nobler traits. Unfortunately, no matter where you go in the world, there are those who through circumstance or preference feel it necessary to prey of the weaknesses of others. But these natural worries about crime and violence become amplified by news outlets and social media feeds that bombard us with horrific stories of hate and division. You should never let fear overpower you to the point you find it impossible to relax and enjoy the world around you. That's what vacations are for, and it's why I wrote this book.

Practicing good situational awareness, whether at home or away, gives you that piece of mind. It allows you to relax and take in all the beauty of your new surroundings while keeping you in tune with your environment. It gives you the ability to recognize patterns and behaviors that signal danger and allows you the space and time you need to avoid violent encounters. That's a pretty handy skill to have, and it's one that doesn't require years of training to master. By simply picking your head up and monitoring baseline behaviors, you change the way you move through and interact with your surroundings, which makes you much less appealing to potential criminals and significantly increases your ability to spot dangerous situations early. Pair that with your natural intuition, and you'll find that situational awareness is a lot more than just "head on a swivel" hypervigilance. It's about mindset, planning, and understanding.

As with any training program, you will get out of this book what you put into it. I've done my best to keep the concepts of situational awareness simple and easy to implement. The more you work through the techniques I've covered, the more you'll notice a difference in the way you read your surroundings. You'll start to pick up on patterns and behaviors that may have gone unnoticed before. Your ability to spot and avoid danger will become instinctive and happen on an almost subconscious level. Getting home safe and sound at the end of a trip away should always be your ultimate goal. If you want to get even deeper into the topic of situational awareness, I recommend reading my first book in the Spotting Danger series, *Spotting Danger Before It Spots You.* That will give you an even greater sense of understanding and a few practical exercises you can use to sharpen your skills. If you plan on traveling with your family, the second and third books in the series, *Spotting Danger Before It Spots Your Kids* and *Spotting Danger Before It Spots Your Teens,* will give the rest of the family a full understanding of the topic and will keep the whole family invested in the security of the group. We all have a role to play when it comes to safety. After all the madness of the last few years, it's time you get back out there and enjoy yourself. Relax and take in all the world has to offer. Whether it's a European vacation or a weekend camping trip, be aware of and engaged with what's happening around you, and do so with the confidence that you can now spot danger before it spots you.

Acknowledgments

If someone had told me five years ago I would one day become an author, I'd have probably thought they were crazy. I've always had plenty to say but writing something worthy of being published always seemed just beyond my reach. Writing, I assumed, was best left to the professionals. It wasn't until I started teaching situational awareness and personal defense courses that I realized there was a considerable gap between the defensive techniques I had learned as a federal air marshal and what was being taught in the civilian world. Often, the information I saw being introduced to the general public assumed a certain level of understanding. Students would sign up for a one-day firearms course or a self-defense seminar and be expected to jump in and keep up regardless of their skill level. In most cases, the information being presented was taught from a strict military or law enforcement perspective and didn't translate well to a civilian class. I'd frequently see students get lost in the barrage of information being presented and fail to achieve what they came there for in the first place: real, sustainable improvements in their performance that could benefit them in their daily lives. I felt that civilian students of self-defense needed something outside of their physical training that could supplement their learning and give them something to refer back to when they needed it, namely, a sound starting point that addressed the complex issues of personal safety from their perspective and on their level. That's when the thought occurred to me, "I should write all this down."

I had no formal guidance or writing experience when I started this journey. I just had a lot of information and lived experiences that I felt could be useful, so I started putting it all down on paper. I wrote about everything from situational awareness and mindset to close-quarters combat techniques and training principles, basically everything I had learned as a federal air marshal, but as it turns out, that was a huge mistake. After sending my manuscript out into the publishing world, I almost immediately began receiving rejection letters. That got me a little down, but I was still determined. It wasn't until I received a letter from YMAA Publication Center that I saw a glimmer of hope. It was still a rejection letter, but this one was different and actually offered me a bit of advice regarding my "extensive" manuscript.

"As a federal air marshal, your superpower seems to be situational awareness, and that's something that everyone can benefit from regardless of what type of self-defense training they pursue. Focus on that topic and resubmit your manuscript."

So that's exactly what I did. I salvaged what I could from the original and started over, now with more focus and a renewed sense of purpose. The result of that effort was a four-book contract with YMAA Publication Center, and the title of "author" now forever attached to my name.

I would have never thought this possible five short years ago, yet here we are. You're currently reading the fourth and final book in my *Spotting Danger* situational awareness series, and I'm still plugging away at my keyboard. For that reason, I would be remiss if I didn't acknowledge all the good people who stayed in my corner and kept me on track during this amazing endeavor.

First and foremost, thank you to my wife and children. You are the reason for everything I do and the source behind many of the stories I put down on these pages. I love you all to the moon and back.

Thank you to my publisher, David Ripianzi, for having faith in my work and guiding me in the right direction. You're the reason these books became a reality, and for that, I will be forever grateful.

To my editor, Doran Hunter, your patience and influence are reflected on every page of these books. You've given me the gift of focus and clarity. Thank you.

Thank you to my publicists, Gene Ching and Barbara Langley. Your hard work and dedication have given me my audience, which continues to grow every day.

To the rest of the staff at YMAA Publication Center, none of this would be possible without such a fantastic crew helping me out. Thank you so much for everything you do.

Thank you to the men and women who risk their lives daily to keep the rest of us free from harm. Your sacrifices may go unseen by many, but I know you're out there holding the line, and I will always be in your corner.

To the writers who have helped guide and inspire me: Lt. Col. David Grossman, Loren Christensen, and Steven Pressfield. Your wisdom and words of encouragement have helped me become a better writer. I appreciate that more than you know.

Thank you to Coach Tony Blauer, who provided the foreword for this book and has been a staple in the self-defense community for decades. Your lessons have kept me from getting my ass kicked on more than one occasion. Keep up the amazing work!

Finally, to my readers, I'm honored and humbled that you've entrusted me with your time. Your safety is important to me. My greatest hope is that you will find something within these pages that benefits you and your family and gives you the confidence that comes from knowing that you are in control of your personal safety. God bless you and thank you from the bottom of my heart.

Appendix——Travel Resources

US State Department—Traveler Information:
https://travel.state.gov/content/travel/en/international-travel/before-you-go/
travelers-with-special-considerations.html

US State Department—STEP Program Registration:
https://step.state.gov/STEP/Pages/Common/Citizenship.aspx

CIA World Fact Book:
https://www.cia.gov/the-world-factbook/

Lonely Planet Travel Guides:
https://www.lonelyplanet.com/

Other Open-Source Information (OSINT):
Google Earth: https://earth.google.com/web/
Yelp: https://www.yelp.com/
Trip Advisor: https://www.tripadvisor.com/
Expedia Travel Resources: https://www.expedia.com/
World Travel Guides: https://www.worldtravelguide.net/city-guides/
CDC and COVID Travel information: https://www.cdc.gov/coronavi-
rus/2019-ncov/travelers/travel-during-covid19.html
World Health Organization Travel Information: https://www.who.int/
emergencies/diseases/novel-coronavirus-2019/travel-advice

Bibliography

Screentime stats:
https://blog.rescuetime.com/screen-time-stats-2018/

Number of inbound international visitors to the United States from 2011 to 2020:
https://www.statista.com/statistics/214686/
number-of-international-visitors-to-the-us/

Terrorism:
https://ourworldindata.org/terrorism

Intel brief:
https://blog.healthadvocate.com/2018/07/communicate-more-effectively-on-your-family-vacation/

Index

About the Author

GARY QUESENBERRY was born in the Blue Ridge Mountains of Virginia. His love of the outdoors and patriotic spirit led him to enlist in the United States Army where he served as an artilleryman during Operation Desert Storm. Gary later became a career federal air marshal where he devoted his life to studying violence and predatory behavior. Now Gary has retired from federal service and serves as the CEO of

Photo by Mary Mcilvaine

Quesenberry Personal Defense Training LLC. There he's developed numerous basic and advanced level training courses focused on mental toughness, and defensive tactics. He has an extensive background in domestic and foreign counterterror training and has worked in both the private and corporate sectors to help educate others on the importance of situational awareness and personal safety. He once again resides in his hometown in Carroll County, Virginia.

www.garyquesenberry.com

BOOKS FROM YMAA

101 REFLECTIONS ON TAI CHI CHUAN
108 INSIGHTS INTO TAI CHI CHUAN
A WOMAN'S QIGONG GUIDE
ADVANCING IN TAE KWON DO
ANALYSIS OF GENUINE KARATE
ANALYSIS OF GENUINE KARATE 2
ANALYSIS OF SHAOLIN CHIN NA 2ND ED
ANCIENT CHINESE WEAPONS
ART AND SCIENCE OF STAFF FIGHTING
THE ART AND SCIENCE OF SELF-DEFENSE
ART AND SCIENCE OF STICK FIGHTING
ART OF HOJO UNDO
ARTHRITIS RELIEF, 3D ED.
BACK PAIN RELIEF, 2ND ED.
BAGUAZHANG, 2ND ED.
BRAIN FITNESS
CHIN NA IN GROUND FIGHTING
CHINESE FAST WRESTLING
CHINESE FITNESS
CHINESE TUI NA MASSAGE
COMPLETE MARTIAL ARTIST
COMPREHENSIVE APPLICATIONS OF SHAOLIN CHIN NA
CONFLICT COMMUNICATION
DAO DE JING: A QIGONG INTERPRETATION
DAO IN ACTION
DEFENSIVE TACTICS
DIRTY GROUND
DR. WU'S HEAD MASSAGE
ESSENCE OF SHAOLIN WHITE CRANE
EXPLORING TAI CHI
FACING VIOLENCE
FIGHT LIKE A PHYSICIST
THE FIGHTER'S BODY
FIGHTER'S FACT BOOK 1&2
FIGHTING ARTS
FIGHTING THE PAIN RESISTANT ATTACKER
FIRST DEFENSE
FORCE DECISIONS: A CITIZENS GUIDE
INSIDE TAI CHI
JUDO ADVANTAGE
JUJI GATAME ENCYCLOPEDIA
KARATE SCIENCE
KATA AND THE TRANSMISSION OF KNOWLEDGE
KRAV MAGA COMBATIVES
KRAV MAGA FUNDAMENTAL STRATEGIES
KRAV MAGA PROFESSIONAL TACTICS
KRAV MAGA WEAPON DEFENSES
LITTLE BLACK BOOK OF VIOLENCE
LIUHEBAFA FIVE CHARACTER SECRETS
MARTIAL ARTS OF VIETNAM
MARTIAL ARTS INSTRUCTION
MARTIAL WAY AND ITS VIRTUES
MEDITATIONS ON VIOLENCE
MERIDIAN QIGONG EXERCISES
MINDFUL EXERCISE
MIND INSIDE TAI CHI
MIND INSIDE YANG STYLE TAI CHI CHUAN
NATURAL HEALING WITH QIGONG
NORTHERN SHAOLIN SWORD, 2ND ED.
OKINAWA'S COMPLETE KARATE SYSTEM: ISSHIN RYU
PRINCIPLES OF TRADITIONAL CHINESE MEDICINE
PROTECTOR ETHIC
QIGONG FOR HEALTH & MARTIAL ARTS 2ND ED.
QIGONG FOR TREATING COMMON AILMENTS

QIGONG MASSAGE
QIGONG MEDITATION: EMBRYONIC BREATHING
QIGONG GRAND CIRCULATION
QIGONG MEDITATION: SMALL CIRCULATION
QIGONG, THE SECRET OF YOUTH: DA MO'S CLASSICS
REDEMPTION
ROOT OF CHINESE QIGONG, 2ND ED.
SAMBO ENCYCLOPEDIA
SCALING FORCE
SELF-DEFENSE FOR WOMEN
SHIN GI TAI: KARATE TRAINING
SIMPLE CHINESE MEDICINE
SIMPLE QIGONG EXERCISES FOR HEALTH, 3RD ED.
SIMPLIFIED TAI CHI CHUAN, 2ND ED.
SOLO TRAINING 1&2
SPOTTING DANGER BEFORE IT SPOTS YOU
SPOTTING DANGER BEFORE IT SPOTS YOUR KIDS
SPOTTING DANGER BEFORE IT SPOTS YOUR TEENS
SPOTTING DANGER FOR TRAVELERS
SUMO FOR MIXED MARTIAL ARTS
SUNRISE TAI CHI
SURVIVING ARMED ASSAULTS
TAE KWON DO: THE KOREAN MARTIAL ART
TAEKWONDO BLACK BELT POOMSAE
TAEKWONDO: A PATH TO EXCELLENCE
TAEKWONDO: ANCIENT WISDOM
TAEKWONDO: DEFENSE AGAINST WEAPONS
TAEKWONDO: SPIRIT AND PRACTICE
TAI CHI BALL QIGONG: FOR HEALTH AND MARTIAL ARTS
THE TAI CHI BOOK
TAI CHI CHIN NA, 2ND ED.
TAI CHI CHUAN CLASSICAL YANG STYLE, 2ND ED.
TAI CHI CHUAN MARTIAL POWER, 3RD ED.
TAI CHI CONCEPTS AND EXPERIMENTS
TAI CHI CONNECTIONS
TAI CHI DYNAMICS
TAI CHI FOR DEPRESSION
TAI CHI IN 10 WEEKS
TAI CHI PUSH HANDS
TAI CHI QIGONG, 3RD ED.
TAI CHI SECRETS OF THE ANCIENT MASTERS
TAI CHI SECRETS OF THE WU & LI STYLES
TAI CHI SECRETS OF THE WU STYLE
TAI CHI SECRETS OF THE YANG STYLE
TAI CHI SWORD: CLASSICAL YANG STYLE, 2ND ED.
TAI CHI SWORD FOR BEGINNERS
TAI CHI WALKING
TAI CHI CHUAN THEORY OF DR. YANG, JWING-MING
TRADITIONAL CHINESE HEALTH SECRETS
TRADITIONAL TAEKWONDO
TRAINING FOR SUDDEN VIOLENCE
TRIANGLE HOLD ENCYCLOPEDIA
TRUE WELLNESS SERIES (MIND, HEART, GUT)
WARRIOR'S MANIFESTO
WAY OF KATA
WAY OF SANCHIN KATA
WAY TO BLACK BELT
WESTERN HERBS FOR MARTIAL ARTISTS
WILD GOOSE QIGONG
WING CHUN IN-DEPTH
WINNING FIGHTS
XINGYIQUAN

AND MANY MORE ...

VIDEOS FROM YMAA

ANALYSIS OF SHAOLIN CHIN NA
ART & SCIENCE OF STAFF FIGHTING
ART & SCIENCE OF STICK FIGHTING
BAGUA FOR BEGINNERS 1 & 2
BAGUAZHANG: EMEI BAGUAZHANG
BEGINNER QIGONG FOR WOMEN 1 & 2
BEGINNER TAI CHI FOR HEALTH
BIOENERGY TRAINING 1 & 2
CHEN TAI CHI CANNON FIST
CHEN TAI CHI FIRST FORM
CHEN TAI CHI FOR BEGINNERS
CHIN NA IN-DEPTH SERIES
FACING VIOLENCE: 7 THINGS A MARTIAL ARTIST MUST KNOW
FIVE ANIMAL SPORTS
FIVE ELEMENTS ENERGY BALANCE
HEALER WITHIN
INFIGHTING
INTRODUCTION TO QI GONG FOR BEGINNERS
JOINT LOCKS
KNIFE DEFENSE
KUNG FU BODY CONDITIONING 1 & 2
KUNG FU FOR KIDS AND TEENS SERIES
LOGIC OF VIOLENCE
MERIDIAN QIGONG
NEIGONG FOR MARTIAL ARTS
NORTHERN SHAOLIN SWORD
QI GONG 30-DAY CHALLENGE
QI GONG FOR ANXIETY
QI GONG FOR ARMS, WRISTS, AND HANDS
QIGONG FOR BEGINNERS: FRAGRANCE
QI GONG FOR BETTER BALANCE
QI GONG FOR BETTER BREATHING
QI GONG FOR CANCER
QI GONG FOR DEPRESSION
QI GONG FOR ENERGY AND VITALITY
QI GONG FOR HEADACHES
QI GONG FOR THE HEALTHY HEART
QI GONG FOR HEALTHY JOINTS
QI GONG FOR HIGH BLOOD PRESSURE
QIGONG FOR LONGEVITY
QI GONG FOR STRONG BONES
QI GONG FOR THE UPPER BACK AND NECK
QIGONG FOR WOMEN WITH DAISY LEE
QIGONG FLOW FOR STRESS & ANXIETY RELIEF
QIGONG MASSAGE
QIGONG MINDFULNESS IN MOTION
QI GONG—THE SEATED WORKOUT
QIGONG: 15 MINUTES TO HEALTH
SABER FUNDAMENTAL TRAINING
SAI TRAINING AND SEQUENCES
SANCHIN KATA: TRADITIONAL TRAINING FOR KARATE POWER
SCALING FORCE
SEARCHING FOR SUPERHUMANS
SHAOLIN KUNG FU FUNDAMENTAL TRAINING 1 & 2
SHAOLIN LONG FIST KUNG FU BEGINNER—INTERMEDIATE—
    ADVANCED SERIES
SHAOLIN SABER: BASIC SEQUENCES
SHAOLIN STAFF: BASIC SEQUENCES
SHAOLIN WHITE CRANE GONG FU BASIC TRAINING SERIES
SHUAI JIAO: KUNG FU WRESTLING
SIMPLE QIGONG EXERCISES FOR HEALTH
SIMPLE QIGONG EXERCISES FOR ARTHRITIS RELIEF
SIMPLE QIGONG EXERCISES FOR BACK PAIN RELIEF
SIMPLIFIED TAI CHI CHUAN: 24 & 48 POSTURES
SIMPLIFIED TAI CHI FOR BEGINNERS 48

SIX HEALING SOUNDS
SUN TAI CHI
SWORD: FUNDAMENTAL TRAINING
TAEKWONDO KORYO POOMSAE
TAI CHI BALL QIGONG SERIES
TAI CHI BALL WORKOUT FOR BEGINNERS
TAI CHI CHUAN CLASSICAL YANG STYLE
TAI CHI CHUAN THEORY OF DR. YANG, JWING-MING
TAI CHI FIGHTING SET
TAI CHI FIT: 24 FORM
TAI CHI FIT: ALZHEIMER'S PREVENTION
TAI CHI FIT: CANCER PREVENTION
TAI CHI FIT FOR VETERANS
TAI CHI FIT: FOR WOMEN
TAI CHI FIT: FLOW
TAI CHI FIT: FUSION BAMBOO
TAI CHI FIT: FUSION FIRE
TAI CHI FIT: FUSION IRON
TAI CHI FIT: HEALTHY BACK SEATED WORKOUT
TAI CHI FIT: HEALTHY HEART WORKOUT
TAI CHI FIT IN PARADISE
TAI CHI FIT: OVER 50
TAI CHI FIT OVER 50: BALANCE EXERCISES
TAI CHI FIT OVER 50: SEATED WORKOUT
TAI CHI FIT OVER 60: GENTLE EXERCISES
TAI CHI FIT OVER 60: HEALTHY JOINTS
TAI CHI FIT OVER 60: LIVE LONGER
TAI CHI FIT: STRENGTH
TAI CHI FIT: TO GO
TAI CHI FOR WOMEN
TAI CHI FUSION: FIRE
TAI CHI QIGONG
TAI CHI PUSHING HANDS SERIES
TAI CHI SWORD: CLASSICAL YANG STYLE
TAI CHI SWORD FOR BEGINNERS
TAI CHI SYMBOL: YIN YANG STICKING HANDS
TAIJI & SHAOLIN STAFF: FUNDAMENTAL TRAINING
TAIJI CHIN NA IN-DEPTH
TAIJI 37 POSTURES MARTIAL APPLICATIONS
TAIJI SABER CLASSICAL YANG STYLE
TAIJI WRESTLING
TRAINING FOR SUDDEN VIOLENCE
UNDERSTANDING QIGONG SERIES
WATER STYLE FOR BEGINNERS
WHITE CRANE HARD & SOFT QIGONG
YANG TAI CHI FOR BEGINNERS
YOQI: MICROCOSMIC ORBIT QIGONG
YOQI QIGONG FOR A HAPPY HEART
YOQI:QIGONG FLOW FOR HAPPY MIND
YOQI:QIGONG FLOW FOR INTERNAL ALCHEMY
YOQI QIGONG FOR HAPPY SPLEEN & STOMACH
YOQI QIGONG FOR HAPPY KIDNEYS
YOQI QIGONG FLOW FOR HAPPY LUNGS
YOQI QIGONG FLOW FOR STRESS RELIEF
YOQI: QIGONG FLOW TO BOOST IMMUNE SYSTEM
YOQI SIX HEALING SOUNDS
YOQI: YIN YOGA 1
WU TAI CHI FOR BEGINNERS
WUDANG KUNG FU: FUNDAMENTAL TRAINING
WUDANG SWORD
WUDANG TAIJIQUAN
XINGYIQUAN
YANG TAI CHI FOR BEGINNERS

AND MANY MORE ...

more products available from . . .

YMAA Publication Center, Inc. 楊氏東方文化出版中心

1-800-669-8892 • info@ymaa.com • www.ymaa.com